VISIT

# Visitors' Delight

## An Anthology of Visitors' Impressions of North Wales

*Edited, with notes and an introduction*
*by*
# Dewi Roberts

*Gwasg Carreg Gwalch*

*ISBN: 0-86381-224-4*

*First published in 1992 by Gwasg Carreg Gwalch,*
*Capel Garmon, Llanrwst, Gwynedd, Wales.*
*☎ 0690 710261*

*Printed in Wales*

**Dewi Roberts, who lives at Denbigh, is actively involved with the promotion of English language writing in Clwyd. He is a member of the Welsh Union of Writers, an associate member of the Welsh Academy, and a founder member of the Gerard Manley Hopkins Society.**

*For Pamela*

# Contents

# Introduction

Holidays in Wales are enjoyed by thousands of visitors each year and tourism is now an important part of the Welsh economy. But tourists to Wales are by no means a twentieth century phenomena, North Wales, which was obviously a very different region in the eighteenth and nineteenth centuries, was attracting its fair share of visitors at that time. The physical discomforts, and indeed hazards, to be encountered by travellers then were such that it is probably difficult for us to envisage such conditions from our own late twentieth century position, when we have become accustomed to travel at speed along the A5 or the A55.

Many of these early visitors recorded their impressions of the region and this book consists of selections from their writings. I have sought to interpret the word visitor in a flexible way to enable me to include not only visitors in the conventional sense but also individuals who have lived in Gwynedd or Clwyd for varying periods of time; Thomas Love Peacock, Gerard Manley Hopkins, and H. G. Wells, for example.

My guiding principle has been the inherent interest of each item. Any attempt to restrict the anthology merely to well known names would have resulted in a far smaller and less interesting selection. In many instances the same visitors will be found in a number of different sections. These sections represent either a specific town, village, or general area.

Much of the material is nineteenth century when, for various reasons, travellers were becoming increasingly conscious of North Wales as an interesting area of Britain to visit.

One of the most interesting features of some of the writing included lies in the way in which it enables us to obtain vivid insights into the personal prejudices of the authors. For example we find Augusta Pearson, in 1853, describing a visit to Caernarfon Castle when one of her companions threw biscuits and raisins from the walls "for the benefit of the dirty little Caernarfon brats".

Readers will find not only personal impressions of visits and periods of residence in the region but also, in a limited number of cases, extracts from fictional works which are at least partly set within its confines.

Many of the writers represented are introduced with a note which serves to put the poem or prose extract which follows in context. In the case of some fairly obscure figures it has not proved possible to obtain information, and even their dates have had to be omitted.

Original spelling has been retained in all items in order to convey the original flavour.

In compiling the selection I have had to resign myself to two seperate limitations.

Firstly, certain well known writers have authenticated associations with North Wales although they do not appear to make specific references to the region in their works. Names which immediately spring to mind include Lewis Carroll, Francis Thompson, Tennyson and Browning.

Secondly, my original concept for the book included material from the last four or five decades. However the works concerned are still in copyright and even if permission had been given by the copyholders the high fees involved would have proved prohibitive.

But despite these omissions we are left with what I hope may prove an interesting assortment of writing by some very varied personalities.

Hopkins summed up the sentiments of many of these when he wrote of

" . . . the woods, waters, meadows, combes, vales,

All the air things wear that build this world of Wales."

My indebtedness is due to the following: to Clwyd County Library Service for launching the book during their 1992 annual festival; Mrs Manon Edwards and her colleagues at Denbigh Library for deploying the resources of the Clwyd libraries; the staff of Clwyd Record Office, Ruthin, for assistance with the illustrative material; and Mr Keverne Smith, of Wrexham, for his encouragement.

*Dewi Roberts*

" . . . the number is so great of sensible, educated men who have written about Wales, or would have written if business or indolence or dislike of fame had not prevented them, that either I find it impossible to visit the famous places . . . or, very rarely, I see that they were imperfect tellers of the truth . . .

Nevertheless, I will please myself and the discerning reader by repeating the names of a few of the places to which I have never been, or of which I will not speak, namely, Llangollen, Aberglaslyn, Betws-y-coed, the Fairy Glen, Capel Curig, Colwyn, Tintern, Bethesda, Llanfairfechan, Llanrhaiadr, Llanynys, Tenby, Mostyn, Glyder Fach and Glyder Fawr, Penmaenmawr, Pen-y-Gader, Pen-y-Gwryd, Prestatyn, Tremadoc, the Swallow Falls, the Devil's Bridge, the Mumbles, Harlech, Portmadoc, Towyn, and Aberdovey . . . I have read many lyrics worse than that inventory."

Edward Thomas : *Beautiful Wales*

# GWYNEDD

## Llandudno

### Mathew Arnold (1822-1888)

*Although some of Arnold's poems, such as "Dover Beach" are still well known, it is primarily as an essayist and critic that he is remembered today. One of his most famous essays, "On the Study of Celtic Literature", takes as its starting point his three week stay at 10 St. George's Crescent, Llandudno, in 1864, which coincided with the National Eisteddfod.*

### From "On the Study of Celtic Literature"

The summer before last I spent some weeks at Llandudno, on the Welsh coast. The best lodging-houses at Llandudno look eastward, towards Liverpool; and from that Saxon hive swarms are incessantly issuing, crossing the bay, and taking possession of the beach and the lodging-houses. Guarded by the Great and Little Orme's Head, and alive with the Saxon invaders from Liverpool, the eastern bay is an attractive point of interest, and many visitors to Llandudno never contemplate anything else. But, putting aside the charm of the Liverpool steamboats, perhaps the view, on this side, a little dissatisfies one after a while; the horizon wants mystery, the sea wants beauty, the coast wants verdure, and has a too bare austereness and aridity. At last one turns round and looks westward. Everything is changed. Over the mouth of the Conway and its sands is the eternal softness and mild light of the west; the low line of the mystic Anglesey, and the precipitous Penmaenmawr, and the great group of Carnedd Llewelyn and Carnedd David and their brethren fading away, hill behind hill, in an aerial haze, make the horizon; between the foot of Penmaenmawr and the bending coast of Anglesey, the sea, a silver stream, disappears one knows not whither. On this side Wales — Wales, where the past still lives, where every place has its tradition, every name its poetry, and where the people, the genuine people, still knows this past, this tradition, this poetry, and lives with it, and clings to it; while, alas, the propserous Saxon on the other side, the invader from Liverpool and Birkenhead, has long ago forgotten his.

But the Celtic genius was just then preparing, in Llandudno, to have its hour of revival. Workmen were busy in putting up a large tent-like wooden building, which attracted the eye of every newcomer, and which my little boys believed (their wish, no doubt, being father to their belief) to be a circus. It turned out, however, to be no circus (for Castor and Pollux) but a temple for Apollo and the Muses. It was the place where the Eisteddfod, or Bardic Congress of Wales, was about to be held; a meeting which has for its object (I quote the words of its promoters) "the diffusion of useful knowledge, the eliciting of native talent, and the cherishing of love of home and honourable fame by the cultivation of poetry, music and art." My little boys were disappointed; but I, whose circus days are over, I, who have a professional interest in poetry, and who, also, hating all one-sidedness and oppression, wish nothing better than that the Celtic genius should be able to show itself to the world and to make its voice heard, was delighted. I took my ticket, and waited impatiently for the day of opening. The day came, an unfortunate one; storms of wind, clouds of dust, an angry, dirty sea. The Saxons who arrived by the Liverpool steamers looked miserable; even the Welsh who arrived by land — whether they were discomposed by the bad morning, or by the monstrous and crushing tax which the London and North-Western Railway Company levies on all whom it transports across those four miles of marshy peninsula between Conway and Llandudno — did not look happy. First we went to the Gorsedd, or preliminary congress for conferring the degree of bard. The Gorsedd was held in the open air, at the windy corner of a street, and the morning was not favourable to open-air solemnities. The Welsh, too, share, it seems to me, with their Saxon invaders, an inaptitude for show and spectacle. Show and spectacle are better managed by the Latin race, and those whom it has moulded; the Welsh, like us, are a little awkward and resourceless in the organisation of a festival. The presiding genius of the mystic circle, in our hideous nineteenth-century costume relieved only by a green scarf, the wind drowning his voice and the dust powdering his whiskers, looked thoroughly wretched; so did the aspirants for bardic honours; and I believe, after about an hour of it, we all of us, as we stood shivering round the sacred stones, began half to wish for the Druid's sacrificial knife to end our sufferings.

# Llandudno

## *Arnold Bennett (1867-1931)*

*Most of Bennett's novels, such as "Clayhanger" and "Anna of the Five Towns", are set in the Potteries, where he was born. One of his most humorous books is "The Card", published in 1911, which is concerned with an enterprising young man, Denry Machin, who dreams of making a fortune. He takes a holiday at Llandudno with two young ladies from his Potteries home town.*

### *From "The Card"*

Ruth chose Llandudno, Llandudno being more stylish than either Rhyl or Blackpool, and not dearer. Ruth and Nellie had a double room in a boarding-house, No.26 St Asaph's Road (off the Marine Parade), and Denry had a small single room in another boarding-house, No.28 St Asaph's Road. The ideal could scarcely have been approached more nearly.

Denry had never seen the sea before. As, in his gayest clothes, he strolled along the esplanade or on the pier between those two girls in their gayest clothes, and mingled with the immense crowd of pleasure-seekers and money-spenders, he was undoubtedly much impressed by the beauty and grandeur of the sea. But what impressed him far more than the beauty and grandeur of the sea was the field for profitable commercial enterprise which a place like Llandudno presented. He had not only his first vision of the sea, but his first genuine vision of the possibilities of amassing wealth by honest ingenuity. On the morning after his arrival he went out for a walk and lost himself near the Great Orme, and had to return hurriedly along the whole length of the Parade about nine o'clock. And through every ground-floor window of every house he saw a long table full of people eating and drinking the same kinds of food. In Llandudno fifty thousand souls desired always to perform the same act at the same time; they wanted to be distracted and they would do anything for the sake of distraction, and would pay for the privilege. And they would all pay at once.

This great thought was more majestic to him than the sea, or the Great Orme, or the Little Orme.

*Denry Machin soon discovers how easy it is to be parted from his money.*

They had not yet discussed finance at all, though Denry would have liked to discuss it. Evidently she regarded him as a man of means. This became clear during the progress of the journey to Llandudno. Denry was flattered, but the next day he had slight misgivings, and on the following day he was alarmed; and on the day after that his state resembled terror. It is truer to say that she regarded him less as a man of means than as a magic and inexhaustible siphon of money.

He simply could not stir out of the house without spending money, and often in ways quite unforeseen. Pier, minstrels, Punch and Judy, bathing, buns, ices, canes, fruit, chairs, rowboats, concerts, toffee, photographs, char-à-bancs: any of these expenditures was likely to happen whenever they went forth for a simple stroll. One might think that strolls were gratis, that the air was free! Error! If he had had the courage he would have left his purse in the house as Ruth invariably did. But men are moral cowards.

He had calculated thus: — Return fare, four shillings a week. Agreed terms at boarding-house, twenty-five shillings a week. Total expenses per week, twenty-nine shillings, — say thirty!

On the first day he spent fourteen shillings on nothing whatever — which was at the rate of five pounds a week of supplementary estimates! On the second day he spent nineteen shillings on nothing whatever, and Ruth insisted on his having tea with herself and Nellie at their boarding-house; for which of course he had to pay, while his own tea was wasting next door. So the figures ran on, jumping up each day. Mercifully, when Sunday dawned the open wound in his pocket was temporarily stanched. Ruth wished him to come in for tea again. He refused — at any rate he did not come — and the exquisite placidity of the stream of their love was slightly disturbed.

*Later in the novel Machin discovers the dangers of life at sea:*

What immediately happened was a storm at sea. He heard it mentioned at Rhyl, and he saw in the deep night, the foam of breakers at Prestatyn. And when the train reached Llandudno, those two girls, in ulsters and capes greeted him with wonderous tales, tales of the storm at sea, and the wrecks, and of lifeboats . . . It was half past nine and half Llandudno was afoot on the Parade and discussing the storm — a storm unparalleled, it seemed, in the month of August. At any rate, people who had visited Llandudno yearly for twenty-five years declared that never had they witnessed such a storm. The new lifeboat had gone forth, amid cheers, about six o'clock to a schooner in distress near Rhos, and at eight o'clock a second lifeboat had departed to the rescue of a Norwegian barque, the Hjalmar round the bend of the Little Orme.

"Lets go to the pier", said Denry. "It will be splendid . . . The pier shook and trembled under the shock of the waves, and occasionally, though the tide was very low, a sprinkle of water flew up and caught their faces. The eyes could see nothing save the passing glitter of the foam on the crest of a breaker. It was the most thrilling situation that any of them had ever been in. And at last came word from the mouths of men who could apparently see as well in the dark as in daylight that the second lifeboat was close to the pier. And then everybody momentarily saw it — a ghostly thing that heaved up pale out of the murk for an instant and was lost again. And the little crowd cheered.

The next moment a Bengal light illuminated the pier, and the lifeboat was silhouetted with strange effectiveness against the storm. And some one flung a rope, and then another rope arrived out of the sea, and fell on Denry's shoulder.

"Haul on there" yelled a hoarse voice. The Bengal light expired. Denry hauled with a will. The occasion was unique and those few seconds were worth to him the whole of Denry's precious life . . . Then two men with beards took the rope from his hands. The air was now alive with shoutings. Finally there was a rush of men down the iron stairway to the lower part of the pier, ten feet nearer the water.

"You stay here, you two" Denry ordered.

"But Denry —"

"Stay here I tell you." All the male in him was aroused. He was off, after the rush of men.

"Half a jiffy," he said, coming back. "Just take charge of this will you?" And he poured into their hands about twelve shillings worth of coppers from his hip pocket. "If anything happens that might sink me," he said and vanished.

It was very characteristic of him, that effusion of calm sagacity in a supreme emergency.

# Conwy

## *Daniel Defoe (1660-1731)*

*Apart from being a pioneer of English fiction, Defoe was one of the earliest journalists and travel writers. His account of his travels around Britain between 1724 and 1726 make fascinating recording, not only because of the description of places visited but also because of the insights we obtain of Defoe's personality.*
*See also under Penmaenmawr, Snowdonia, Bangor, Holywell, St Asaph and Vale of Clwyd.*

### *From "Tour Through the Whole Island of Great Britain"*

Conwy is the poorest but pleasantest town in this county for the bigness of it: it is seated on the bank of a fine river, which is not only pleasant and beautiful, but is a noble harbour for ships, had they any occasion for them there: the stream is deep and safe, and the river broad, as the Thames at Deptford. It only wants a trade suitable to so good a port, for it infinitely outdoes Chester or Liverpool itself.

# Conwy

## *Richard Warner (1763-1857)*

*Richard Warner undertook two pedestrian tours of the region. He was a cleric from Bath, and his accounts make interesting, frequently amusing reading.*
*Warner gives the following lively account of the crossing of the river Conwy.*
*See also under Holywell, Abergele, Snowdonia.*

### *From "A Second Walk Through North Wales" (1798)*

Arriving at length at the passage-house, we discovered the tide was out, and that we could not get to Conwy unless we chose to cross the sands to the channel of the river, about three quarters of a mile distant, where a boat was in waiting to receive passengers. On our expressing some doubts as to the safety of this expedition at night and without a guide, the man at the passage observed, with a sarcastic grin, that if we were expeditious we should overtake a party who would act both as guides and protectors to us — three *old women* crossing to Conwy with butter and eggs. Ashamed at

*Conwy*

being thought unequal to any undertaking of these antiquated females, we immediately pursued the direction they had taken; but not withstanding our expedition could not reach them before they had crossed a brook in the sands, by wading through it, after pulling off their stockings and shoes, and tucking up their petticoats to the middle. Here our courage failed us; we enquired, therefore, of these amphibious ladies whether or not there were a safer place for crossing the brook. They answered, that a quarter of a mile lower down it might be avoided entirely, but desired us to make haste as the tide was rapidly coming in. Following their direction, we soon found ourselves in the midst of a wild waste of sand, which, thrown into ridges by the undulation of the water, had the appearance of a solid sea. The light of the moon, not sufficient to render any of the surrounding objects visible, reflected a faint ray upon this expanse alone, which gave an air of desolation to it that filled the imagination with the most awful fancies. Nor were these dissipated by the conviction of real danger, arising from the treachery of the sands, which occasionally gave way under our feet, and the flowing tide that closely followed our footsteps. At length, with considerable difficulty, we gained the boat, were ferried to Conwy, and soon reached our old quarterts — the "Bull's Head".

# Conwy

## *W. Hutton*

*Hutton recalls the days when it was not possible to traverse the Conwy by bridge, and ferry boats conveyed travellers from one shore to the other.*
*Se also under St Asaph.*

### *From "Remarks Upon North Wales, being the Result of Sixteen Tours of the Principality" (1803)*

I must now cross the river Conwy, about half a mile over. I was sorry that my poor horses must be flogged into a boat, for, to inflict punishment, without a fault, indicates brutality of mind. At a very small expence, the entrance might be made easy and expeditious, without the whip, or the hazard of a limb. This I pointed out to the boatmen, but might as well have addressed the boat. Old habits, though bad, are still favourite habits.

# Conwy

## *Thomas Gray (1716-71)*

*This is one of the three principal poems by which Gray is remembered today, the others being "Elegy written in a Country Churchyard" and "Ode on a Prospect of Eton College". Here he writes of a hypothetical situation and uses this to full poetic affect. He writes of Edward I's slaughter of the native Welsh poets following his conquest of Wales. "The Bard" fired the imagination of many of Gray's contemporaries, making them eager to visit North Wales.*

### *"The Bard"*

'Ruin seize thee, ruthless King!
Confusion on thy banners wait!
Tho' fann'd by Conquest's crimson wing
They mock the air with idle state.
Helm, nor hauberk's twisted mail,
Nor e'en thy virtues, tyrant, shall avail
To save thy secret soul from nightly fears,
From Cambria's curse, from Cambria's tears!
— Such were the sounds that o'er the crested pride

18

Of the first Edward scatter'd wild dismay,
As down the steep of Snowdon's shaggy side
He wound with toilsome march his long array :—
Stout Glo'ster stood aghast in speechless trance;
'To arms!' cried Mortimer, and couch'd his quivering lance.

On a rock, whose haughty brow
Frowns o'er old Conwy's foaming flood,
Robed in the sable garb of woe
With haggard eyes the Poet stood;
(Loose his beard and hoary hair
Stream'd like a meteor to the troubled air)
And with a master's hand and prophet's fire
Struck the deep sorrows of his lyre:
'Hark, how each giant oak and desert-cave
Sighs to the torrent's awful voice beneath!
O'er thee, O King! their hundred arms they wave,
Revenge on thee in hoarser murmurs breathe:
Vocal no more, since Cambria's fatal day,
To high born Hoel's harp, or soft Llewellyn's lay.


# Aber

## *Julius Rodenberg (1831-1914)*

*Rodenberg was German, having been born in Hessen. Following his university studies he visited several European countries. He became one of the most distinguished journalists in Germany in the late nineteenth century and also wrote poems, stories, travel books and literary criticism.*

*During his extended visit to Wales in 1856 he stayed on a farm at Aber, situated between Bangor and Conwy, and used this as the base for his excursions. Here he gives us an insight into his sense of morality.*

*See also under Betws-y-coed, Corwen.*


### *From "An Autumn in Wales"*

In these mountain regions the weather changes amazingly quickly; after that golden autumn afternoon, a storm had now blown up which roused the sea in its depths and hurled the thick clouds against the rocks so that they streamed with rain. I tarried and eventually, facing rain and storm, came home late but this time without accident, as evening moonlight showed me the way. Everyone at the farm was already in bed; only Sarah still sat by the kitchen fire. I rebuked myself that she had had to watch and wait so long on my account.

'Oh no, not just on your account', said Sarah, 'I wouldn't have gone to bed yet.'

I wished her goodnight and went upstairs. But hardly had I reached my little room than down below I heard the soft sound of first the kitchen door and then the house door. Curiosity aroused, I went to the window and, in the light of the moon that to my advantage was veiled by the clouds, saw Sarah going over the yard and to the half-open door of a shed from which crept out a figure that — as it stood up — appeared to be none other than — Owen. Truly, I thought, it wasn't only on my account that she had remained sitting up so long! I hoped to be able to be a witness of a Welsh pastoral scene in storm and rain; but I had deceived myself, for the Phyllis of my farm had devised things more comfortably. She came back again across the yard, her faithful shepherd behind her, then into the house and into the kitchen. But how my astonishment grew when, instead of sobs, oaths and kisses, I heard only a sound which indicated that Owen was taking off his boots and Sarah her shoes. And truly — in stocking feet they came up the stairs, past my chamber and into Sarah's little room opposite!

'No!' I cried out — 'that's too much! that goes beyond the bounds of decency! that's unheard of! This girl of barely eighteen, with her childish eyes and modest behaviour, shy in speech and conduct — Celts, Celts — I should have known that it's in their blood. But what's that to me? Perhaps we are still living in a paradise here, where the serpent has not yet spoken!'

# Llanrwst

## *Williams Bennett*

### *From "The Pedestrian Guide Through North Wales" (1837)*

I proceeded to Llanrwst, but halted upon the bridge to take a view of the Conwy (over which beautiful river its arches expand), and the town to which it leads. I was here accosted by an old man, who asked me, "if I should like to feel the bridge shake?" As I answered in the affirmative, he desired me to place my back against the side over the centre arch, and striking the opposite parapet rather heavily with his own, a tremulous motion was distinctly felt; on this account, it is called the Shaking Bridge. It was built in 1636, from a plan of the celebrated Inigo Jones, and cost £1000, which was defrayed by the counties of Denbighshire and Caernarvonshire, which it unites.

Llanrwst is built upon the Denbighshire side of the river, The Three Eagles is the most commodious inn in the town; and, being rather fatigued, I threw my limbs upon a sofa, and resigned myself to the drowsy god, first taking especial care to order a substantial repast to be in readiness for me on my return from the land of Nod. My last waking recollection was the words of Mr Lover's favourite song,

"There's no use at all in my going to bed,
For it's dreams and not sleep, that comes into my head."

Dreams, however, did not picture my slumbers, and I awoke to the unrivalled delight of a weary and hungry traveller — an excellent hot dinner.

# Llanrwst

## *A. G. Bradley*

*A. G. Bradley was a very popular travel writer early in this century, and his other prolific titles include "Highways and Byways of South Wales". His often idiosyncratic comments on people and places make interesting reading, although one wonders how many readers he has today?*
*See also under Bangor, Abererch, Corwen.*

### *From "Highways and Byways of North Wales" (1898)*

Llanrwst is a typical old fashioned Welsh town of some 3,000 souls, contained for the most part in a single long street, which terminates in an old and picturesque market place . . . Once upon a time it was famous for its harps. And how old it is may be gathered from the statement in the Gwidir Chronicle that grass grew in its streets after the desolation of the Glyndŵr wars and the deer grazed through them . . . Gwydir Castle is close by and all upon our route, which passing out of the town crosses the river by one of the many famous bridges in North Wales. The merit of this

*Llanrwst church*

one might lie in the complete charm of its situation, and the buoyant transparency of the broad river, which rushes through its arches. But it chooses rather to urge a doubtful claim to Inigo Jones, who was a doubtful native of Llanrwst, as its designer, and to vaunt a singular capacity for shaking when struck smartly on the parepet above its centre. There is generally a loafer about who, for the price of a pint of beer, is only too anxious and willing to convince the sceptical upon this point, the last performer whom I witnessed banging his back against the wall in the interests of truth and science was, I was assured, the remains of an Oxford M.A., who was reduced to this means of satisfying an unquenchable thirst.

# Llanrwst

## Mrs Rodolph Stowell

*The arrival of the motor car transformed travel. Mrs Stowell appears to be one of the earliest motorists to record her travels in Wales, and her account appeared in 1908. See under Rhuddlan.*

### From "Motor Tours in Wales and the Border Counties"

There are a good many interesting things here — things much older than the church itself; but not the least pleasing, I think, is the Latin epitaph that the former rector composed, with a pretty wit, for his own tomb. It has been thus translated:—

"Once the undeserving schoolmaster,
Then the more undeserving lecturer,
Last of all the most undeserving rector of this parish.
Do not think, speak, or write anything evil of the dead."

If we are going to Rhuddlan it will not be necessary for us to cross the shaking bridge, designed — perhaps — by Inigo Jones. I see no object in a bridge shaking, myself, but there are always those at hand who for a consideration will shake you the bridge if it gives you pleasure.

# Penmaenmawr

## Daniel Defoe (1660-1731)

*See notes under Conwy, Snowdonia, Bangor, Holywell, St Asaph, The Vale of Clwyd.*

### From "A Tour Through the Whole Island of Great Britain"

. . . we went over the famous precipice called Penmen-muir, which indeed fame has made abundance more frightful, than it really is; for though the rock is indeed very high, and if any one should fall from it, it would dash them in pieces, yet, on the other hand, there is no danger of their falling; and besides, there is now a wall built all the way, on the edge of the precipice, to secure them.

# Penmaenmawr

## *Dr Samuel Johnson (1709-1784)*

*Dr Johnson's tour of North Wales was undertaken in 1774. His friends the Thrales were directly responsible for this visit, and while in the region Johnson kept a fairly detailed account of his impressions.*
*See also under Denbigh and St Asaph.*

### *From "A Diary of a Journey into North Wales in the year 1774"*

In our way from Bangor to Conwy, we passed again the new road upon the edge of Penmaen Mawr, which would be very tremendous, but that the wall shuts out the idea of danger. In the wall are several breaches, made, as Mrs Thrale very reasonably conjectured, by fragments of rocks which roll down the mountain, broken perhaps by frost, or worn through by rain.

# Penmaenmawr

## *William Roscoe (1753-1831)*

*Roscoe played a prominent role in the public life of Liverpool in the early 19th century. He represented the city in Parliament and wrote on political matters, including the slave trade. He also wrote a biography of Lorenzo de Medici, and even found time to devote to a piece for children "The Butterfly's Ball and the Grasshopper's Feast".*
*See under Beddgelert, Snowdonia, Betws-y-coed.*

### *From "Wanderings and Excursions in North Wales 1853"*

I pursued the road following the sweep of the coast towards Penmaen Mawr, whose rocky, precipitous base, running out in a bluff promontory, projects into the waves. In the course of the afternoon, while pausing on an eminence to contemplate the features of the landscape, I beheld at a distance a vast rainbow, stretching its purple-tinged radius from shore to shore. It was a glorious spectacle. The contrast of the many-coloured bow with the dark waters, the sparkling clearness of the sky above, the brightness of the sunshine resting on the surrounding hills, and the

*Penmaenmawr*

various features of the nearer scenery formed altogether so magnificent a scene, that even the traveller in the grander regions of the Valais or Savoy can seldom witness anything more sublime.

It was towards nightfall when I approached that part of my journey where the road, hewn out of the solid rock, was like a terrace midway along the face of the mountain, many hundred feet above the sea, which breaks in thunder below. The evening was mild and beautiful. Clouds, slightly charged with lightning, hung over sea and land; and from time to time bright flashes, unaccompanied by thunder, kindled the firmament, — showing momentarily the form of the clouds, and gleaming over the face of the ocean. Occasionally the eye caught, by this transient light, glimpses of the black, beetling rocks overhanging the road, communicating to them a gloomy grandeur of character which I should in vain endeavour to describe. Formerly, before the road had been widened, and defended by a parapet, this passage of Penmaen Mawr was full of danger. But, though terrific, it is now perfectly safe; unless we contemplate the possibility of the rain or frost detaching, as it sometimes does, vast rocky fragments of the superincumbent mountain, and hurling them headlong upon the helpless traveller. Ideas of such catastrophes naturally enough present themselves, in such situations, to the mind; it was therefore not without pleasure that I found myself beyond the possibility of danger.

Correctly speaking, this great mountain promontory has two divisions, — one of which is called Penmaen Mawr, the other Penmaen Bach, — the latter lying the nearest to Conwy; but the whole is generally known to the tourist by the former name. Less than a century ago, a narrow zigzag path, along the side of the rock, was the only convenience for travellers.

At that time there was an inn at each end of the pass, and the witty Dean Swift is said to have composed the following couplets, which greeted the admiring traveller on the sign-posts as he entered and debouched from it:—

"Before you venture here to pass,
Take a good refreshing glass."

"Now you're over take another,
Your drooping spirits to recover."

It was from the many accidents which occurred that the Legislature was induced, in 1772, to assist in carrying out the plan projected by Mr John Sylvester, and in forming the present grand terrace, which has more recently been further enlarged and improved under the direction of Mr Telford. It is well guarded on the sea side, and many of the overhanging fragments of rock have been blasted.

# Penmaenmawr

## *Charles Tennyson Turner (1808-1879)*

*Turner was the elder brother of Alfred, Lord Tennyson. He collaborated with Alfred in a volume entitled "Poems of Two Brothers". He changed his name in 1830 on inheriting the estate of a great-uncle. He wrote some three hundred sonnets, which were brought together in 1880 in "Collected Sonnets, Old and New".*

### *"The Artist on Penmaenmawr*

That first September day was blue and warm,
Flushing the shaly flanks of Penmaenmawr;
While youths and maidens, in the lucid calm
Exulting, bathed or bask'd from hour to hour;

What colour-passion did the artist feel!
While evermore the jarring trains went by,
Now, as for evermore, in fancy's eye,
Smutch'd with the cruel fires of Abergele;
Then fell the dark o'er the great crags and downs,
And all the night-struck mountain seem'd to say,
'Farewell! these happy skies, this peerless day!
And these fair seas — and fairer still than they,
The white-arm'd girls in dark blue bathing-gowns,
Among the snowy gulls and summer spray.'

*Charles Tennyson Turner*

# Betws-y-coed

## *Julius Rodenberg (1831-1914)*

*There are times when Rodenberg is sympathetic to the Welsh, as in the extract below
concerning a visit to the Swallow Falls and an encounter with a local lady, who acts as an
unofficial guide.*
*See under Corwen, Aber.*

### *From "An Autumn in Wales"*

The waterfall appeared in all the splendour of the setting sun; compared
with the Benglog Falls this seemed to us like a park, surrounded not by
bare and sinister rocks but by infinitely charming and varied scenery,
though with a certain wildness. The contrast of the rushing water, lit by
the setting sun, with the dark mass of the pool below, was a pleasant
surprise to the eye. Up in the wood the lady with the hat and green silk
parasol was waiting for us.

'Sir, you will remember me!' she said. 'Don't forget me, Sir!'

'No', I said, 'I won't forget you. I will keep you in my thoughts.'

But that was not what was meant. The lady wanted money.

'What for, then?' I asked. 'A man needs to know, what for?'

'Because you have seen the waterfall, Sir!' she replied.

'Who's given you the waterfall on lease then?'

'The dear God who made it has given it to me on lease', she answered
calmly. It was no good — we had to give her money.

'The crazy woman!' cried one of the Englishmen.

'The shameless creature!' cried the other.

I thought her neither crazy nor shameless. If the kings in the Middle Ages fenced in the forests and placed a ban on the rivers, why should not a poor Welshwoman have the idea of levying a toll on a natural beauty of her native country? It is a good thing that as yet there are not many such barriers to free viewing; I had a lot of trouble in pacifying the infuriated Englishmen.

# Betws-y-coed

## Theodore Watts Dunton (1832-1914)

*Born in Huntingdonshire, this poet, novelist and critic is now almost a forgotten name. He was associated with many of the Pre-Raphaelites and was a friend of George Borrow, with whom he shared a close interest in gipsy life.*

*This preoccupation can be clearly seen in his novel Aylwyn, published in 1898, much of which is set in a highly romanticised Snowdonia and from which the passages below describing Betws-y-coed are taken.*

### From "Aylwyn"

I need not describe my journey to North Wales. On reaching Bettws y Coed I turned into the hotel there — 'The Royal Oak' — famished; for, as fast as trains could carry me, I had travelled right across England, leaving rest and meals to chance. I found the hotel full of English painters, whom the fine summer had attracted thither as usual. The landlord got me a bed in the village. A six-o'clock *table d'hôte* was going on when I arrived, and I joined it. Save myself, the guests were, I think, landscape painters to a man. They had been sketching in the neighbourhood. I thought I had never met so genial and good-natured a set of men, and I have since often wondered what they thought of me, who met such courteous and friendly advances as they made towards me in a temper that must have seemed to them morose or churlish and stupid.

One day as Sinfi and I were strolling through the lovely glades between Capel Curig and Bettws y Coed on our way to a fishing-place, we sat down by a stream to eat some bread and cheese we had brought with us.

The sunlight, as it broke here and there between the thick foliage, was playing upon the little cascades in such magical fashion — turning the

*Pont-y-pair, Betws-y-coed*

water into a torrent that seemed as though molten rubies and sapphires and opals were ablaze in one dancing faery stream, — that even the dark tragedy of human life seemed enveloped for a moment in an atmosphere of poetry and beauty.

*The central character searches the area for a loved one.*

Weeks passed by. I visited all the scenes that were in the least degree associated with Winnie.

The two places nearest to me — Fairy Glen and the Swallow Falls — which I had always hitherto avoided on account of their being the favourite haunts of tourists — I left to the last, because I specially desired to see them by moonlight. With regard to Fairy Glen, I had often heard Winnie say how she used to go there by moonlight and imagine the Tylwyth Teg or the fairy scenes of the *Midsummer Night's Dream* which I had told her of long ago — imagine them so vividly that she could actually see, on a certain projecting rock in the cliffs that enclose the dell, the figure of Titania dressed in green, with a wreath of leaves round her head. And with regard to the Swallow Falls, I remembered only too well her telling me, on the night of the landslip, the Welsh legend of Sir John Wynn, who died in the seventeenth century, and whose ghost,

29

imprisoned at the bottom of the Falls on account of his ill deeds in the flesh, was heard to shriek amid the din of the waters. On that fatal night she told me that on certain rare occasions, when the moon shines straight down the chasm, the wail will become an agonised shriek. I had often wondered what natural sound this was which could afford such pabulum to my old foe, Superstition. So one night, when the moon was shining brilliantly — so brilliantly that the light seemed very little feebler than that of day — I walked in the direction of the Swallow Falls.

Being afraid that I should not get much privacy at the Falls, I started late. But I came upon only three or four people on the road. I had forgotten that my own passion for moonlight was entirely a Romany inheritance. I had forgotten that a family of English tourists will carefully pull down the blinds and close the shutters, in order to enjoy the luxury of candle-light, lamp-light, or gas, when a Romany will throw wide open the tent's mouth to enjoy the light he loves most of all — 'chonesko dood', as he calls the moonlight. As I approached the Swallow Falls Hotel, I lingered to let my fancy feast in anticipation on the lovely spectacle that awaited me. When I turned into the wood I encountered only one person, a lady, and she hurried back to the hotel as soon as I approached the river.

Following the slippery path as far as it led down the dell, I stopped at the brink of a pool about a dozen yards, apparently, from the bottom, and looked up at the water. Bursting like a vast belt of molten silver out of an eerie wilderness of rocks and trees, the stream, as it tumbled down between high walls of cliff to the platform of projecting rocks around the pool at the edge of which I stood, divided into three torrents, which themselves were again divided and scattered by projecting boulders into cascades before they fell into the gulf below. The whole seemed one wide cataract of living moonlight that made the eyes ache with beauty.

# Betws-y-coed

## *William Roscoe (1753-1831)*

*See note under Penmaenmawr, Beddgelert, Snowdonia.*

### *From "Wanderings and Excurtions in North Wales" (1853)*

The sun rose with a June splendour over the village of Bettws y Coed, dispersing the light haze which hung over those far-stretching plantations of luxuriant larch-trees, that distinguished it from every other place I had seen in the Principality. These graceful trees which in the early season of the year are almost the first to greet his ray in their spring dress of lively green, are here ranged in serried lines of richest verdure along the valley, and feather the mountain sides to their loftiest summits. The broad beam which in the early morning seemed to gush, like a gentle flood, over a meadow of these trees, with their lancet tops gracefully bending to meet his approach, became shivered into a thousand particles of light by the contact, circulating round their pensile branches, revealing the transparent fibres and delicate hues of their tasselled leaves.

I had made my head-quarters at the Royal Oak, which I can recommend for its homely comforts, and the active services of the little obliging *grisette*, who never lets the traveller wait long for his savoury brakfast of eggs and ham, a quality which I take to be one of no small consequence in this land, where long mountain-walks and many roads at all times provide him with a craving appetite. The alluring sunshine, and the health-inspiring breeze of the morning, were calling me forth, and I had besides the time-hallowed castle ruins of Dolwyddelan, the Conway Falls, and I knew not what of interest and beauty.

# Beddgelert

## *William Spencer (1769-1834)*

An important feature of the popular culture of the nineteenth century was the ballad. The now almost forgotten William Spencer contributed to this genre with his ballad based on the very well known legend of Gelert. The creation of this myth appears to be due largely to the fertile imagination of an eighteenth century local innkeeper named Pritchard.

The legend relates how Llywelyn, Prince of Gwynedd, set out one day from his palace in Beddgelert for a day's hunting. He left behind him his infant son and his hound Gelert. On his return he discovered the cot to be empty and bloodstained.

O'erturned his infants bed he found
With bloodstained covert rent
And all around, the walls and ground
With recent blood bespent.

He called his child, no voice reply'd
He searched with terror wild
Blood, blood he found on every side
But nowhere found his child.
'Hell hound! my child's by thee devoured'
The frantic father cry'D
And to the hilt his vengeful sword
He plunged in Gelert's side.

The dog's dying bellow is answered by the cries of the infant, who is alive. Shortly afterwards Llywelyn comes upon the body of a large wolf and he is consumed by remorse. Gelert had fought off the wolf when it attacked the princes' heir. Llywelyn never smiled again.

Ah, what was then Llewelyn's pain
For now the truth was clear
His gallant hound the wolf had slain
To save Llewelyn's heir.

Vain vain was Llewelyn's woe.
'Best of thy kind, adieu,
The frantic blow which laid you low
This head shall ever rue.'

# Beddgelert

## *William Roscoe (1753-1831)*

*See note under Penmaenmawr, Snowdonia.*

### *From "Wanderings and Excursions in North Wales" (1853)*

The pleasant site of Beddgelert, in the heart of these bold romantic hills — its smooth green meadows and pleasant streams, its sylvan beauty, and the rich contrast of the scenes by which it is surrounded, with its many varied objects of interest sufficient to amuse every taste — came more fresh upon the mind and the eye after the agreeable excitement of my recent wanderings. It was here, after many days of long and toilsome ramble among the Carnarvonshire hills, I was prepared truly to enjoy a brief repose, although I never felt less weary than when I wound my way along the river to the spot where the three valleys meet. It had the same serene and quiet pastoral look as when I visited it years before; and it was with renewed pleasure that I watched the murmuring confluence of the Gwynant and the Colwyn; and the river Glaslyn, formed by these streams, afterwards flowing through scenery highly romantic, beyond the wild falls and rocky breaks which surround Pont Aber-Glaslyn.

The afternoon of my arrival at Beddgelert was devoted to the enjoyment of its hospitable cheer with a few fellow-pedestrians I there met, to the luxury of repose, and the pleasure of unexpectedly spending it with a companion of my school days. We had a delightful little banquet, at which social wit and good humour presided, with that pleasant idleness one most enjoys after laborious toil, whether physical or intellectual.

# Beddgelert

## *Michael Faraday (1791-1867)*

*Faraday's claim to fame rests with his discovery of electro-magnetic induction, which led directly to the electric generator and motor.*
*In 1819, when he was a young man, Faraday toured North Wales and recorded detailed impressions of the visit.*
*See also under Snowdonia.*

### *From "Journal of a Tour Through North Wales"*

' . . . we got on towards Cardigan Bay and soon saw it over the mountain tops. Snowdon also came into view but much obscured by clouds. We tramped along, delighted by all we saw, passed over the hill heads, crossed Pont-Aber-Glaslyn, an astonishing pass up in the mountains, soon ascended to Bethgelert and fixed ourselves at the great Inn.

Having washed and taken tea we roamed out in the village, a very pretty romantic place at the foot of Snowdon. It takes its name from Gelert, the greyhound, Bethgelert the grave of Gelert. The story of the hound destroying a wolf that came in to a cottage whilst human assistance was absent and saving the life of Prince Llewellyn's child and afterward being slain by the Prince who supposed too hastily the dog had killed his son, is known to everyone. The poor dog's grave is in a field by the Church and marked by a large stone and the Master of the Inn where we put up has a fine large greyhound in memory of the event which is honored by the name of Gelert.

It was here too I heard the first Welsh Harper. During our meal we were entertained by the exertion of one on his instrument. He was now a middle aged blind man who sitting at the foot of the stairs played to the whole house as in former times. His harp was large, of the usual form but of very cheap materials. Most of the Inns in North Wales have a harper belonging to them as a necessary appendage and I now expect to be often amused by their efforts. Tomorrow we go over Snowdon. Goodnight.'

# Beddgelert

## *Edward Thomas (1878-1917)*

*Edward Thomas was born in London, but his parental roots were in Wales. Although he is remembered mainly as a poet, he only began writing verse in earnest some three years prior to his premature death. He was also the author of a substantial amount of prose, especially on rural subjects. His book on Wales was published in 1905. "Beautiful Wales" presents a highly romanticised view of the principality. See also under Nefyn, Dolgellau & Cader Idris, Bala.*

### *From "Beautiful Wales*

Here he writes of a man who:

. . . returning from Beddgelert fair by a gloomy road, saw a great and splendid house conspicuously full of gaiety in a place where no such house had seemed to stand before; and supposing that he had lost his way, he asked and was given a lodging, and found the chambers bright and sounding with young men and women and children, and slept deeply in a fine room, on a soft white bed, and on waking and studying his neighbourhood, saw but a bare swamp and a tuft of rushes beneath his head.

# Snowdonia

## *Daniel Defoe (1660-1731)*

*See notes under Conwy, Penmaenmawr, Bangor, Holywell, The Vale of Clwyd.*

### *From "Tour Through the Whole Island of Great Britain"*

Snowdon Hill is a monstrous height and according to its name, had snow on the top in the beginning of June; and perhaps had so until the next June, that is to say, all the year. These impassable heights were doubtless the refuges of the Britains, when they made continual war with the Saxons and Romans, and retreated on occasion of their being over powered, into these parts where, in short, no enemy could pursue them . . . The principal town in this part is Caernarvon, a good town, with a castle built by Edward I to curb and reduce the wild people of the mountains and secure the passage into Anglesey.

Welsh mountains are indeed so like the Alps, that except the language of the people, one could hardly avoid thinking he is passing from Grenoble to Susa . . . The lakes also, which are so numerous here, make the similitude the greater, nor are the fables which the country people tell of these lakes much unlike the stories which we meet with among the Switzers of the famous lakes of their country.

# Snowdonia

## *William Bingley (1774-1823)*

*Like Bennett and certain other travellers in North Wales Bingley was not content to confine his observations merely to the beauty of the landscape. He was also concerned with the figures in that landscape. Some of his observations about the Welsh make interesting and amusing reading. See under Cwm Bychan.*

### *From "North Wales: Scenery, Antiquities, Customs: 1798-1801"*

In those mountainous, or secluded parts of the country, that are scarcely known to the English tourist, where their manners still retain the greatest degree of originality, the lower class of the inhabitants appear to possess an innocence and simplicity of character, unknown in the populous parts of our own country; and amongst these it is, that we are to search for that native hospitality, so much boasted of by the Welsh writers: but, wherever the English have had frequent communication, from their being in general so profuse of their money, and from the temptation that this has afforded to practice impositions on them, I have found the people but little different from the like class amongst us. On the great roads, they seem to take a pride in over reaching, in most of their little bargains, their Saxon neighbours . . . A Welsh gentleman informed me that it is a common practice among them to ask nearly as much more for an article as they mean to take, and with those who know them it is always usual to offer them less. This is the case, in some measure, in our own country, but certainly not as frequently as in Wales.

# Snowdonia

## *Rev. R. H. Newell*

### *From "Letters on the Scenery of Wales" (1821)*

Many go up to see the sun-rise, and are disappointed. Your view would probably be finer in a bright noon. The prospect is of course vast, and almost unbounded; but surely its character may be understood from an inferior elevation; and what is gained by *fancying* you see a speck, which the guide *tells* you is the Isle of Man? If you prefer the certainty of nearer views, the appearance of the mountain itself will gratify you more: the caverns, lakes, precipices, and other peculiar features, are exceedingly grand and curious. I remember one of them that we came upon suddenly, about half way up, with which I was much pleased. A crater, perhaps a quarter of a mile in circumference, and of tremendous depth, with steep smooth sides sloping inwards to the bottom without a single break. On peeping over the edge, I could discern two diminutive lakes, appearing in the deep gloom below, like two gems, and one of them of a pure emerald colour.

*Dolbadarn castle*

# Snowdonia

### *William Roscoe (1753-1831)*

*See notes under Penmaenmawr, Beddgelert, Betws-y-coed.*

### *From "Wanderings and Excursions in North Wales" (1853)*

Dolbadern was the central fortress of those commanding the passes into Anglesea and Caernarvonshire. It is built in a circular shape with hard, laminated stone, cemented with strong mortar. The inner diameter measures twenty-six feet, its height is between eighty and ninety, and the thickness of its walls nearly eight. It appears to have had three stories, besides the vaulted basement used as a dungeon; and the broken steps by which I ascended showed that the communication was by a spiral staircase. That it stood many an attack, the tumulus of loose stones at the foot of the lower lake, and other remains of ancient fortifications, offer a sufficient proof. It was accessible only by a single causeway. By whom it was founded, or at what period, must still remain a subject of conjecture.

Mr Pennant considers it the work of some Welsh prince, from whom, with the surrounding ground, it took its name; its erection, in this case, may be referred to the eighth or ninth century. The seat of feudal violence or revenge, a succession of hapless victims immured within its dungeon often filled the adjacent hills and valleys with cries of distress. Among these, Prince Owen, called Owen Gôch, the Red, was held captive by his brother Llewellyn, against whom he had combined with his younger brother. They were defeated in a sanguinary conflict, and Owen paid the penalty of twenty years' solitary captivity in this tower. In the wars of Glendower it frequently changed masters, being always considered one of the master-keys into the interior of Snowdonia. Its ruins are now spread over the entire summit of the bold projecting rock, exposing to view the massy foundations of the exterior building, and the site of its once terrific donjon.

# Snowdon

## *J. M. W. Turner (1775-1851)*

*The following short quotation was included in the catalogue of the Royal Academy Exhibition in 1800, in which Turner exhibited a picture of Dolbadarn Castle.*
*Owain Goch, the brother of Llywelyn the Great, was imprisoned at the castle for twenty years because he challenged his brothers inheritance. When Edward I conquered Wales he obtained his freedom.*

How aweful is the silence of the waste,
Where nature lifts her mountains to the sky.
Majestic solitude behold the tower
Where hopeless Owen, long imprison'd pin'd,
And wrung his hands for liberty in vain.

# Snowdonia

## *Michael Faraday (1791-1867)*

*See also under Beddgelert.*

### *From "Journal of a Tour Through North Wales"*

The shades of evening now began to gather over us and we all sank as if by agreement into a very quiet sober state in which we should have continued perhaps for the rest of our ride had not the expertness and agility of a blind woman roused us. Poor Bess was waiting in the road for the coaches for there were two, our and another immediately behind it, and on hearing the noise of the wheels slipped a little on one side. When they were up to her she ran to the hinder part and feeling for the wheels or the steps got hold of the irons and immediately mounted despite of the coach's motion or her blindness. She and the guard appeared to be old friends but we soon found her object was to sell her goods. She pulled out some Welsh wigs knitted by herself and offered them to the passengers behind for sale, pleading her blindness as a strong reason why they should purchase. I bought one of the Welsh wigs in remembrance of the old woman and gave 1/6d for it. She then pulled out some socks on which I scolded her for not producing them before. They were a shilling a pair and I wanted to take them instead of the wig, but she was not willing even though I offered her the eighteen penny wig for the shilling socks, and we found afterwards from the guard to whom she confessed her reason that the wigs were her own knitting but the socks she only sold for a neighbour. She then stretched across the coach to the front passengers but they would not buy and afterwards she clung to the side of the vehicle standing on the spring between the wheel and the body of the coach and peeping (query) it at the window offered her articles for sale there, but there were boys only and they did not want socks or Welsh wigs. Finding further stay on our coach useless she descended and avoiding the horses of the coach immediately behind us got round it and mounted in the same manner as she had done with us. But I am afraid all her exertions did not gain her any further success at this time for she soon after got down and went off home.

# Snowdonia

## *William Wordsworth (1770-1850)*

*Book 13 of Wordsworth's autobiographical poem "The Prelude" begins with an account of Robert Jones, a close friend, and himself climbing Snowdon on a moonlit summer night. He began "The Prelude" in the 1790's and revised it as late as the 1840's. There are considerable differences between the various versions and the extract below is from the version completed in 1806.*

*See notes under Caernarfon, Llangollen.*

### *From "The Prelude"*

In one of these excursions, travelling then
Through Wales on foot, and with a youthful Friend,
I left Bethkelet's huts at couching-time,
And westward took my way to see the sun
Rise from the top of Snowdon. Having reach'd
The Cottage at the Mountain's Foot, we there
Rouz'd up the Shepherd, who by ancient right
Of office is the Stranger's usual guide;
And after short refreshment sallied forth.

It was a Summer's night, a close warm night,
Wan, dull and glaring, with a dripping mist
Low-hung and thick that cover'd all the sky,
Half threatening storm and rain; but on we went
Uncheck'd, being full of heart and having faith
In our tried Pilot. Little could we see
Hemm'd round on every side with fog and damp,
And, after ordinary travellers' chat
With our Conductor, silently we sank
Each into commerce with his private thoughts:
Thus did we breast the ascent, and by myself
Was nothing either seen or heard the while
Which took me from my musings, save that once
The Shepherd's Cur did to his own great joy
Unearth a hedgehog in the mountain crags
Round which he made a barking turbulent.
This small adventure, for even such it seemed

In that wild place and at the dead of night,
Being over and forgotten, on we wound
In silence as before. With forehead bent
Earthward, as if in opposition set
Against an enemy, I panted up
With eager pace, and no less eager thoughts.
Thus might we wear perhaps an hour away,
Ascending at loose distance each from each,
And I, as chanced, the foremost of the Band;
When at my feet the ground appear'd to brighten,
And with a step or two seem'd brighter still;
Nor had I time to ask the cause of this,
For instantly a Light upon the turf
Fell like a flash: I looked about, and lo!
The Moon stood naked in the Heavens, at height
Immense above my head, and on the shore
I found myself of a huge sea of mist,
Which, meek and silent, rested at my feet:
A hundred hills their dusky backs upheaved
All over this still Ocean, and beyond,
Far, far beyond, the vapours shot themselves,
In headlands, tongues, and pormontory shapes,
Into the Sea, the real Sea, that seem'd
To dwindle, and give up its majesty,
Usurp'd upon as far as sight could reach.
Meanwhile, the Moon look'd upon this shew
In single glory, and we stood, the mist
Touching our very feet; and from the shore
At distance not the third part of a mile
Was a blue chasm; a fracture in the vapour,
A deep and gloomy breathing-place through which
Mounted the roar of waters, torrents, streams
Innumerable, roaring with one voice.
The universal spectacle throughout
Was shaped for admiration and delight,
Grand in itself alone, but in that breach
Through which the homeless voice of waters rose,
That dark deep thoroughfare had Nature lodg'd
The Soul, the Imagination of the whole.

# Snowdonia

## *Charles Darwin (1809-1882)*

*Darwin, Marx, and Freud are among the most influential modern thinkers. Darwin's account of his early life in his "Autobiography" makes interesting reading, as here where he describes a visit to North Wales while he was a student at Cambridge. The object of the excursion was to examine the geological phenomena of the region.*

## *From the "Autobiography"*

Next morning we started for Llangollen, Conway, Bangor and Capel Curig. This tour was of decided use in teaching me a little how to make out the geology of a country. Sedgwick often sent me on a line parallel to his, telling me to bring back specimens of the rocks and to mark the stratification on a map. I have little doubt that he did this for my good, as I was too ignorant to have aided him. On this tour I had a striking instance how easy it is to overlook phenomena, however conspicuous, before they have been observed by anyone. We spent many hours in Cwm Idwal, examining all the rocks with extreme care, as Sedgwick was anxious to find fossils in them; but neither of us saw a trace of the wonderful glacial phenomena all around us; we did not notice the plainly scored rocks, the perched boulders, the lateral and terminal moraines. Yet these phenomena are so conspicuous that, as I declared in a paper published many years afterwards in the *Philosophical Magazine*, a house burnt down by fire did not tell its story more plainly than did this valley. If it had still been filled by a glacier, the phenomena would have been less distinct than they now are.

At Capel Curig I left Sedgwick and went in a straight line by compass and map across the mountains to Barmouth, never following any track unless it coincided with my course. I thus came on some strange wild places and enjoyed much this manner of travelling. I visited Barmouth to see some Cambridge friends who were reading there, and thence returned to Shrewsbury and to Maer for shooting; for at that time I should have thought myself mad to give up the first days of partridge-shooting for geology or any other science.

*Darwin did not enjoy the best of health and at a later stage of his life returned to North Wales.*

*Llanberis Pass*

In the summer of 1842 I was stronger than I had been for some time and took a little tour by myself in N. Wales, for the sake of observing the effects of the old glaciers which formerly filled all the larger valleys. I published a short account of what I saw in the *Philosophical Magazine*. This excursion interested me greatly, and it was the last time I was ever strong enough to climb mountains or to take long walks, such as are necessary for geological work.

# Snowdonia

### *Michael Faraday (1791-1867)*

*See note under Beddgelert.*
*Here Faraday writes of the peasant women of the region.*

### *From "Journal of a Tour Through North Wales"*

They are bare legged and bare footed, sometimes bare headed. Their cloaths are coarse and hang loosely and they have not the appearance at first, (at least they had not to me), of being remarkable for cleanliness or order. But this erroneous judgment must be rectified. In their houses and their persons, they are equally orderly and the very custom of walking bare legged and footed is a proof of it. Every girl and woman in going from their houses to the town takes her shoes and if she has stockings, them also with her. She walks however without them on, but on nearing the town washes her feet in a brook, puts herself in order and then makes a respectable appearance.

The mistress of the hut into which we had entered was sitting on a low stool knitting and surrounded by her family, a stout chubby boy and two little girls. One of them an infant was ill and the others were trying to amuse it or administering to its wants. The woman with all the care she had could still entertain pity for us and showed her sorrow at the weather in a very expressive manner. Her little boy gave us seats and took my hat and then retired to the window and we talked with each other and the woman with her little ones each set smiling when by some easy word they found the other was speaking of them. Another traveller, a man of the country, came up whilst we were there and she asked him also to come in seeming to mind nothing how much trouble she caused herself nor how much we dirty her clean house, but he rested himself in the porch which ornamented the door. When the storm had subsided we prepared to be gone and the woman appeared astonished when we offered her anything like recompense to her little boy for the trouble we had given her. We left them very happy ourselves and they very much surprised.

# Snowdonia

## Richard Warner

*See under Conwy, Holywell, Abergele.*
*Warner and his walking companions find themselves lost in the hinterlands of Gwynedd.*

### From "A Second Walk Through North Wales" (1798)

. . . Still we kept on, and still without success, till perplexed by intersecting roads, which every step grew less perceptible, we at length found ourselves at the top of a mountain, perfectly at a loss how to proceed. Rambling on for some time, we discoverd a solitary cottage . . . to this we directed our steps and were fortunate enough to find the family at home, consisting of a man, his wife, and sister. The first spoke a little English; and (after understanding from whence we came and whither we were going) informed us we had wandered considerably out of our road . . . During the whole of this conversation, we could not avoid remarking that the woman appeared to be very uneasy; but when he offered to accompany us a little way in order to put us into the right road the distress of both was more perceptible, and the wife in particular seemed, by her gestures, to entreat him not to leave her. To these marks of anxiety, however, he only answered "nonsense, nonsense", and extricating himself from the ladies who held him by the arm and coat he joined our party. On our enquiring the cause of this evident alarm on the part of the females, he informed us that our appearance had awakened their fears; that they had assured him we were either travelling robbers or prisoners who had broken from gaol; that the packs on our backs were full of the plunder we had picked up, and without doubt we should rob and murder him when we had seduced him from his dwelling.

J . . . n had taken with him from home a map of North Wales and a small pocket compass, and it was now we found their utility and importance. By showing and explaining these to our conductor, he marked out what course we were to make for, since everything like a path had long since faded away, and nothing but untrodden heath was before us. We therefore rewarded the confidence of our guide with a handsome present, and took leave of him; who, after giving us very particular directions, many blessings, and shaking us heartily by the hand, (a token of kindness which these mountaineers never fail to offer) committed us to the wild hills of Merionethshire.

# Snowdonia

## *Louisa Costello*

*See under Maentwrog, Hawarden.*
*Mrs Costello has some interesting comments on the Welsh and their remote homes in the Gwynedd hills.*

### *From "Falls, Lakes and Mountains in North Wales" (1839)*

They are, in regard to strangers, strictly honest, exceedingly civil, and attentive, and rarely give occasion for complaint. This we found throughout our journey, though we seldom heard any praises bestowed on them by their countrymen. In the wildest parts of the mountains the people are said to be very dirty and slovenly, sullen, and unwilling to oblige; but as they speak only Welsh, and few travellers give themselves the trouble to learn their language, the supposed incivility complained of may arise from other causes. In the towns and villages carelessness is sufficiently apparent if not actual want of cleanly habits; the streets are always infested with pigs, and a dung-heap is generally exhibited at the door, as unseemly as in any French town: but no one can accuse the Welsh of neglecting the outward appearance of their houses, for their devotion to whitewash is such, that, as I have before had occasion to remark, both walls and roof are often as white as the most profuse application of the brush could make them, to the entire destruction of the picturesque.

# Snowdonia

## *George Borrow (1803-1881)*

*Borrow is perhaps the most frequently read of all writers on Wales. His "Wild Wales" is a classic of travel literature. Published in 1862 it records a walking tour through the principality eight years earlier.*
*See also under Wrexham.*

### *From "Wild Wales" (1862)*

After staying about an hour at Caernarvon we started for Llanberis, a few miles to the east. Llanberis is a small village situated in a valley, and takes its name from Peris, a British saint of the sixth century, son of Helig ab Glanog. The valley extends from west to east, having the great mountain of Snowdon on its south, and a range of immense hills on its northern, side. We entered this valley by a pass called Nant y Glo or the ravine of the coal, and passing a lake on our left, on which I observed a solitary coracle, with a fisherman in it, were presently at the village. Here we got down at a small inn, and having engaged a young lad to serve as guide, I set out with Henrietta to ascend the hill, my wife remaining behind, not deeming herself sufficiently strong to encounter the fatigue of the expedition.

Pointing with my finger to the head of Snowdon towering a long way from us in the direction of the east, I said to Henrietta:

"Dacw Eryri, yonder is Snowdon. Let us try to get to the top. The Welsh have a proverb: 'It is easy to say yonder is Snowdon; but not so easy to ascend it.' Therefore I would advise you to brace up your nerves and sinews for the attempt."

We were far from being the only visitors to the hill this day; groups of people, or single individuals, might be seen going up or descending the path as far as the eye could reach. The path was remarkably good, and for some way the ascent was anything but steep. On our left was the vale of Llanberis, and on our other side a broad hollow, or valley of Snowdon, beyond which were two huge hills forming part of the body of the grand mountain, the lowermost of which our guide told me was called Moel Elia, and the uppermost Moel y Cynghorion. On we went until we had passed both these hills, and come to the neighbourhood of a great wall of rocks constituting the upper region of Snowdon, and where the real difficulty of the ascent commences. Feeling now rather out of breath we sat down on a little knoll with our faces to the south, having a small lake near us, on our left hand, which lay dark and deep, just under the great wall.

Here we sat for some time resting and surveying the scene which presented itself to us, the principal object of which was the north-eastern side of the mighty Moel y Cynghorion, across the wide hollow or valley, which it overhangs in the shape of a sheer precipice some five hundred feet in depth. Struck by the name of Moel y Cynghorion, which in English signifies the hill of the counsellors, I inquired of our guide why the hill was so called, but as he could afford me no information on the point I presumed that it was either called the hill of the counsellors from the Druids having held high consultation on its top, in time of old, or from the unfortunate Llewelyn having consulted there with his chieftains, whilst his army lay encamped in the vale below.

Getting up we set about surmounting what remained of the ascent. The path was now winding and much more steep than it had hitherto been. I was at one time apprehensive that my gentle companion would be obliged to give over the attempt; the gallant girl, however, persevered, and in little more than twenty minutes from the time when we arose from our resting-place under the crags, we stood, safe and sound, though panting, upon the very top of Snowdon, the far-famed Wyddfa.

The Wyddfa is about thirty feet in diameter and is surrounded on three sides by a low wall. In the middle of it is a rude cabin in which refreshments are sold, and in which a person reside throughout the year, though there are few or no visitors to the hill's top, except during the months of summer. Below on all sides are frightful precipices except on the side of the west. Towards the east it looks perpendicularly into the dyffrin or vale nearly a mile below, from which to the gazer it is at all time an object of admiration, of wonder and almost of fear.

There we stood on the Wyddfa, in a cold bracing atmosphere, though the day was almost stiflingly hot in the regions from which we had ascended. There we stood enjoying a scene inexpressibly grand, comprehending a considerable part of the main land of Wales, the whole of Anglesey, a faint glimpse of part of Cumberland; the Irish Channel, and what might be either a misty creation or the shadowy outline of the hills of Ireland. Peaks and pinnacles and huge moels stood up here and there, about us and below us, partly in glorious light, partly in deep shade. Manifold were the objects which we saw from the brow of Snowdon, but of all the objects which we saw, those which filled us with most delight and admiration, were numerous lakes and lagoons, which, like sheets of ice or polished silver, lay reflecting the rays of the sun in the deep valleys at his feet.

# Snowdonia

## *Charles Kingsley (1819-1875)*

*This cleric, essayist, and poet is perhaps best remembered today as the author of the children's classic "The Water Babies".*

*"Two Years Ago", published in 1857, is set partly in Snowdonia, with which the author appears to have been very familiar. In this extract we are presented with a character in the grip of despair, and the author evokes his stress in the context of the wild, rugged, threatening landscape.*

*See The Dee, Porthmadog.*

### From "Two Years Ago"

Elsley left the door of Pen-y-gwryd, careless whither he went, if he went only far enough.

In front of him rose the Glyder Vawr, its head shrouded in soft mist, through which the moonlight gleamed upon the chequered quarries of that enormous desolation, the dead bones of the eldest-born of time. A wild longing seized him; he would escape up thither; up into those clouds, up anywhere to be alone — alone with his miserable self. That was dreadful enough: but less dreadful than having a companion — ay, even a stone by him — which could remind him of the scene which he had left; even remind him that there was another human being on earth beside himself. Yes — to put that cliff between him and all the world! Away he plunged from the high road, splashing over boggy uplands, scrambling among scattered boulders, across a stormy torrent bed, and then across another and another: — when would he reach that dark marbled wall, which rose into the infinite blank, looking within a stonethrow of him, and yet no nearer after he had walked a mile?

He reached it at last, and rushed up the talus of boulders, springing from stone to stone; till his breath failed him, and he was forced to settle into a less frantic pace. But upward he would go, and upward he went, with a strength which he never had felt before. Strong? How should he not be strong, while every vain felt filled with molten lead; while some unseen power seemed not so much to attract him upwards, as to drive him by magical repulsion from all that he had left below?

So upward and upward ever, driven on by the terrible gad-fly, like Io of old he went; stumbling upwards along torrent beds of slippery slate, writhing himself upward through crannies where the waterfall splashed cold upon his chest and face, yet could not cool the inward fire; climbing, hand and knee up cliffs of sharp-edged rock; striding over downs where huge rocks lay crouched in the grass, like fossil monsters of some ancient world, and seemed to stare at him with still and angry brows. Upward still, to black terraces of lava, standing out hard and black against the gray cloud, gleaming, like iron in the moonlight, stair above stair, like those over which Vathek and the princess climbed up to the halls of Eblis. Over their crumbling steps, up through their cracks and crannies, out upon a dreary slope of broken stones, and then — before he dives upward into the cloud ten yards above his head — one breathless look back upon the world.

On the right hand Snowdon rises. Vast sheets of utter blackness — vast sheets of shining light. He can see every crag which juts from the green walls of Galt-y-Wennalt; and far past it into the Great Valley of Cwm Dyli; and then the red peak, now as black as night, shuts out the world with its huge mist-topped cone. But on the left hand all is deepest shade. From the highest saw-edges where Moel Meirch cuts the golden sky, down to the very depths of the abyss, all is lustrous darkness, sooty, and yet golden still. Let the darkness lie upon it for ever! Hidden be those woods where she stood an hour ago! Hidden that road down which, even now, they may be pacing home together! — Curse the thought! He covers his face in his hands and shudders in every limb.

He lifts his hands from his eyes at last: — what has befallen?

Before the golden haze a white veil is falling fast. Sea, mountain, lake, are vanishing, fading as in a dream. Soon he can see nothing but the twinkle of a light in Pen-y-gwryd, a thousand feet below; happy children are nestling there in innocent sleep. Jovial voices are chatting round the fire. What has he to do with youth, and health, and joy? Lower, lower ye clouds! Shut out that insolent and intruding spark, till nothing be seen but the silver sheet of Cwm Fynnon, and the silver zig-zag lines which wander into it among black morass, while down the mountain side go, softly sliding, troops of white mist-angels. Softly they slide, swift and yet motionless, as if by some inner will, which needs no force of limbs; gliding gently round the crags, diving gently off into the abyss, their long white robes trailing about their feet.

# Ffestiniog

## *George Lyttleton (1709-73)*

*Lyttleton, who numbered among his friends Henry Fielding and Alexander Pope, became leader of the opposition when Walpole was prime minister.*
*On a visit to Wales the Vale of Ffestiniog made a considerable impression on him.*

### *From "A Gentleman's Tour Through Monmouthshire and Wales" (1774)*

With the woman one loves, with the friend of one's heart, and a good study of books one might pass an age in this vale and think it a day. If you have a mind to live long and renew your youth, come and settle in

Ffestiniog. Not long ago there died in that neighbourhood an honest Welsh farmer, who was 106 years of age. By his first wife he had thirty children, ten by his second, four by his third, and was saved by two concubines; his youngest son was eighty one years younger than his eldest, and 800 descended from his body, attended his funeral.

# Ffestiniog

## *Mr Pratt*

*The author describes a winter day, when he was glad to seek the shelter and warmth of a public house.*

### *From "Gleanings Through Wales, Holland, and Westphalia" (1798)*

The snow had drizzled for about half an hour, but more radiant sunshine succeeded; yet the frost was so much stronger than the thaw that the flakes encrusted on my hat and clothes as they fell, and I was as complete an icicle on my return to the inn as any of the surrounding objects.

The surrounding objects, indeed, on my return were in perfect contrast to those without doors. The whole peasantry of Ffestiniog appeared to be got into the public house, where the blazing hearth and vacant hilarity set frost and snow at defiance. These happy groups are very frequent in North Wales, and particularly in those seasons when the rigorous elements drive men more upon their internal resources. This indeed was an extraordinary occasion. The Member for Merioneth, in which county stands this sweet village, had given a fat sheep, and a barrel of home brewed to the poor of every parish within his district to counteract the inclemancy of the frost; and this animal was roasting whole in the kitchen, while the guests, in blissful expectation, were gathered together in a room adjoining. All that could beat an alarm to appetite, or give to appetite gratified its most perfect tranquility, was at work . . .

# Ffestiniog

## 'A Barrister'

*In 1811 a work with the somewhat lengthy title "A Tour in Quest of Geneaology through Several Parts of Wales, Somersethire, and Wiltshire" was published. The authorship is merely attributed to 'A Barrister'.*

*He was invited during his tour to the home of a most hospitable host near Ffestiniog, who related a legend concerning a nearby lake.*

'Our dinner was now announced; the trout was delicious, and we could not avoid remarking their colour approaching that of salmon in full season.

"This is nothing", said my host, "to what the fish of a more distant lake exhibit, of a much deeper red and higher flavour, and yet no wonder when we trace the origin of this superior excellence by traditional lore."

It is said that in the first colonization of the country, the men of a certain mountain district, wanting the indispensable means of providing for population seized the females of a neighbouring province and carried them off; but being pursued, a bloody battle took place, in which the ravishers fell, and the violated ladies, whose affections they had won, resolving not to survive their gallants and their disgrace, in the glow of injured honour, a little subdued by the delicate blush of a softer passion, rushed into a neighbouring lake, which has ever since been called by a name commemorative of the event, Llyn y Morwynion, The Maidens Lake, where, if they were not fairly metamorphosed into trout, they had the reputation at least of having given them their colour.'

# Maentwrog

## Louisa Costello

*Mrs Costello, whom we may assume to be a fairly typical English upper class tourist of her period, reveals quite a lot about her own prejudices in recording her visit to North Wales. See also under Hawarden, Snowdonia.*

### From "Falls, Lakes and Mountains in North Wales" (1839)

There are two waterfalls within a walk of Maentwrog, both fine when the season allows them sufficient water; but it is generally worth while to take the walk which has a fall for its object, as it rarely happens that the scenery does not repay you. Hitherto we had not seen, in any instance, a specimen of Welsh character which led us to believe the assertion, that the people are artful and deceitful; but it was left to a pretty innocent-looking boy whom we took as our guide, to prove that such traits exist. As he found we were disposed to linger for some time in the wood of the Rhaiaidr Du, he invented an excuse, which we readily admitted, and, after securing his gratuity, left us to join, as he told us, a carpenter who was busy making a new gate which we had passed: the man having as he informed us, with rather a piteous look, requested him, in Welsh, to go back and assist him, while we remained at the water-fall. On our return we saw the hero of his tale indeed, and had some conversation with him, but our young traitor of the smooth tongue had taken good care not only to avoid partaking of his toil, but had gone merrily back to Maentwrog, to lie in wait for others who would, no doubt, select him, as we had done, from his fellows, for the frankness and simplicity of his countenance. The Welsh peasants have the reputation, amongst the better order, of being singularly false and never speaking their minds, concealing under an air of extreme candour great art and remarkable selfishness. If this be true, they are worthy descendants of their countrymen of old, who betrayed their chiefs, and those chiefs each other, upon all occasions when, to be true, would have been dangerous to their own interests. This solitary instance of falsehood is, however, all that gave me reason to mistrust the people, and assuredly their civility and apparent readiness to oblige are infinitely more to be remarked.

# Maentwrog

## Gerard Manley Hopkins (1844-1889)

*The following short poem by Hopkins was written at Maentwrog, a village situated between Harlech and Ffestiniog.*
*He was on holiday at the time, and already much attracted to the beauty of the Welsh landscape, which he later celebrated so memorably during his period as a theology student in Clwyd.*
*See under St Asaph, Rhyl, The Elwy Valley, Denbigh.*

### At a Welsh Waterfall

It was a hard thing to undo this knot.
The rainbow shines, but only in the thought
Of him that looks. Yet not in that alone.
For who makes rainbows by invention?
And many standing round a waterfall
See one bow each, yet not the same to all,
But each a hand's breadth further than the next.
The sun on falling waters writes the text
Which yet is in the eye or in the thought.
It was a hard thing to undo this knot.

# Caernarfon

## Sir Richard Colt Hoare (1758-1838)

*This antiquary was a Wiltshire man and the author of an ancient history of the county.*
*He was a keen traveller with an interest in fine art and made drawings of many of the places which he visited.*
*See also under Llangollen, Denbigh.*

### From "The Journeys of Sir Richard Colt Hoare through England and Wales: 1793-1810"

30th June, 1797:
Dull country, fields enclosed with stone walls etc. Church of Lanbublic [*Llanbeblig*] on right, a large building, the parish church of Carnarvon.

Descend to Carnarvon. Cross the river. Road good. In the midst of hay harvest. The roads in general much improved and still improving in many of the most unfrequented parts of Wales; done by subscription and county rates. Well planned. Women bare-footed and employed in knitting.

Carnarvon: a neat town, chiefly built within the precincts of the old walls. The castle: large, massive pile of building, rather too much so to make it picturesque. A good view of it at a little distance up the river. Its chief trade in slates, of two colours, blue and of a rich purple. Over the entrance to the castle is a figure of its founder, King Edward. Good view from the summit of the Eagle Tower, so called from the sculpture of a bird on its summit; part of it still remaining but mutilated . . .

A magnificent hotel has been lately built at the extremity of the town by Lord Uxbridge. Commands a fine view of the River Menai and the opposite coast of Anglesey. Very flat. Number of vessels continually passing up and down with the tide enliven the view. The landlord comes from Cheshire and has taken the inn on trial. The little concourse of travellers will, I fear, impede his success as innkeeper. He rents a large farm and has introduced the culture of turnips which answer well. Cheap bill.

[Bill at the Hotel Carnarvon
2 large place of salmon
2 fowls
Neck of mutton
Veal cutlets
Peas-beans-potatoes
2 lobsters
Gooseberry tart
For the above we were charged eight shillings]

# Caernarfon

## William Wordsworth (1770-1850)

*It is though that this poem was written at Caernarfon Castle.*
*See under Snowdonia, Llangollen.*

### Sonnet: Composed among the ruins of a Castle in North Wales
### (September 1824)

Through shattered galleries, 'mid roofless halls,
Wandering with timid footsteps oft betrayed,
The Stranger sighs, nor scruples to upbraid
Old Time, though he, gentlest among the Thralls
Of Destiny, upon these wounds hath laid
His lenient touches, soft as light that falls,
From the wan Moon, upon the towers and walls,
Light deepening the profoundest sleep of shade,
Relic of Kings! Wreck of forgotten wars,
To winds abandoned and the prying stars,
Time *loves* Thee! at his call the Seasons twine
Luxuriant wreaths around thy forehead hoar;
And, though past pomp no changes can restore,
A soothing recompense, his gift, is thine!

*William Wordsworth*

# Caernarfon

## Augusta Pearson

*Augusta Pearson was one in a long line of middle and upper class English tourists to Wales in the nineteenth century. Her visit took place in August 1853, when she was seventeen, and, as so often in the case of these visitors, her personal prejudices are clearly revealed.*

### From "A Spinsters Tour of North Wales" (1853)

#### Thursday, August 18th
'Up early, walked to the post in a very hopeful state of mind, returned, dejected and spiritless, even a tour in North Wales is improved by the occasional receipt of a letter; *ésperons toujours*. At 1.15 we set off per train

to Carnarvon, did not take an umbrella, and so of course down came the rain, but we got into some old windows of the Castle and sketched for more than an hour. I fancy we must have had rather a comical effect in our niches aloft, for I observed the different people point us out as part of the show to their less observant companions.

This is another of Edwards 1st's castles, making the third we have seen in the last few days. Those Welsh mountaineers were well protected at all events. We had a little collation in the ruins, consisting of biscuits and raisins which Charles got at a grocer's, and what we could not eat, he flung down from the Castle for the benefit of the little dirty Carnarvon brats. Before leaving this dull and *unclean* town we strolled down to the pier, where I was very much amused watching the proceedings of the people waiting to cross in the ferry boat. There was one nice little Welshwoman, the very pink of neatness, she was attired in the blue plaid of the country with a cap as white as snow and her hat which crowned it, was most cannily enveloped in a blue pocket handkerchief — to keep the sea water from it, I suppose. She sat there on the boat with the composure of a little Duchess but no drawing of mine could do the little dear justice. The rest of the assemblage were of quite a different order, men, who had evidently been taking a holiday and taking a little something besides, which just elevated their spirits, sufficiently to make them amusing, and their stupid faces and gesticulations as they harangued the company were irresistibly ridiculous.'

# Porthmadog and Tremadog

## *Thomas Love Peacock (1785-1866)*

*Peacock, who was born at Weymouth, initially visited Wales in 1810. He stayed at Tremadoc and then at Maentwrog. There he met the daughter of the local parson, Jane Gryffydd, who later became his wife.*

*While staying at Tremadoc in 1810 he saw something of attempts being made by the famous William Maddock to reclaim land from the sea by the building of an embankment. When he came to write his novel Headlong Hall Peacock drew on his observations.*

### *From "Headlong Hall"*

'They now emerged, by a winding ascent, from the Vale of Llanberis, and after some little time arrived at Beddgelert. Proceeding through the sublimely romantic pass at Aberglaslyn, their road led to the edge of Traeth Maur, a vast arm of the sea, which they then beheld in all the magnificence of the flowing tide. Another five miles brought them to the embankment, which has since been completed, and which, by connecting the two counties of Meirionnydd and Caernarvon, excluded the sea from an extensive tract. The embankment, which was carried on at the same time from both the opposite coasts, was then very nearly meeting in the centre. They walked to the extremity of that part of it which was thrown out from the Caernarvonshire shore. The tide was now ebbing: it had filled the vast basin within, forming a lake about five miles in length and more than one in breadth . . . As they looked upwards with their backs to the open sea, they beheld a scene which no other in this country can parallel, and which the admirers of the magnificence of nature will ever remember . . . Vast rocks and precipices, intersected with little torrents, formed the barrier on the left: on the right, the triple summit of Moelwyn reared its majestic boundary: in the depth was that sea of mountains, the wild and stormy outline of the Snowdonian chain, with the giant Wyddfa towering in the midst . . . The tide ebbed with rapidity: the waters within, retained by the embankment, poured through its two points an impetuous cataract, curling and boiling in innumerable eddies, and making a tumultuous melody admirably in unison with the surrounding scene. The three philosophers looked on in silence; and at length unwillingly turned away, and proceeded to the little town of Tremadoc, which is built on land recovered in an similar manner from the sea. After inspecting the manufactories, and refreshing themselves at the inn on a cold saddle of mutton and a bottle of sherry, they retraced their steps towards Headlong Hall, commenting as they went on the various objects they had seen.'

# Porthmadog and Tremadog

## *P. B. Shelley (1792-1822)*

*Shelley lived in Gwynedd for approximately one year. He was a young man when he came to Tremadog in 1811 and had made himself unpopular in certain quarters because of his political radicalism. (He was, for instance, an anti-monarchist). Shelley was wildly enthusiastic about William Maddock's land reclamation scheme, which he supported with passion, but was shocked by the poverty of the Welsh people.*

*A full account of this very turbulent period in the poets' life will be found in Richard Holmes' fine biography "Shelley the Pursuit", published in 1974. Here are some extracts from Shelley's letters written from Tremadoc.*

"This country of Wales is excessively grand. Rocks piled on each other to tremendous heights, rivers formed into cataracts by their projections, and valleys clothed with woods present an appearance of enchantment. But why do they enchant? Why is a mountain more affecting than a plain? Thus does knowledge lose all pleasure by attempting to arrest the fleeting phantom. Nature here is marked with the most impressive character of loveliness. Once I was tremendously alive to tones and scenes, but the habit of analysing feelings, I fear, does not agree with me."

"The scenery is more strikingly grand in the way from Capel Curig to our house than ever I beheld. The road passes the foot of Snowdon. All around you see lofty peaks lifting their summits far above the clouds, wildly wooded valleys below, and dark tarns reflecting every tint and shape of the scenery above them."

"The Society in Wales is very stupid. They are all aristocrats and saints; but that I don't mind in the least. The unpleasant part of the business is that they hunt people to death who are not likewise."

"Cambria is the last refuge of the most vulgar prejudices of aristocracy. Lawyers of unexampled villainy rule, and grind the poor whilst they cheat the rich. The peasants are mere serfs and are fed and lodged worse than pigs."

*The North Wales Gazette reported an eloquent and passionate speech which Shelley made at a public meeting in support of William Maddock's ambitious project to reclaim land from the sea.*

"The Embankment at Tremadoc is one of the noblest works of human power — it is an exhibition of human nature as it appears in its noblest and natural state — benevolence — it saves, it does not destroy. Yes! the unfruitful sea once rolled where human beings now live and earn their honest livelihood. Cast a look around these islands, through the perspective of these times — behold famine driving millions even to madness; and own how excellent, how glorious, is the work which will give no less than three throusand souls the means of competence. How can anyone look upon that work and fail to join me, when I here publicly pledge myself to spend the last shilling of my fortune, and devote the last breath of my life to this great, this glorious cause."

# Porthmadog and Tremadog

## *Charles Kingsley (1819-1875)*

*See under Snowdonia, The Dee.*

### *From "Two Years Ago."*

The pleasant summer voyage is over. The *Waterwitch* is lounging off Port Madoc, waiting for her crew. The said crew are busy on shore drinking the ladies' healths, with a couple of sovereigns which Valentia has given them, in her sister's name and her own. The ladies, under the care of Elsley, and the far more practical care of Mr Bowie, are rattling along among children, maids, and boxes, over the sandy flats of the Traeth Mawr, beside the long reaches of the lazy stream, with the blue surges of the hills in front, and the silver sea behind. Soon they begin to pass wooded knolls, islets of rock in the alluvial plain. The higher peaks of Snowdon sink down behind the lower spurs in front; the plain narrows; closes in, walled round with woodlands clinging to the steep hillsides; and, at last, they enter the narrow gorge of Pont-Aberglaslyn — pretty enough, no doubt, but much over-praised; for there are in Devon alone a dozen passes far grander, both for form and size.

Soon they emerge again on flat meadows, mountain-cradled; and the grave of the mythic greyhound, and the fair old church, shrouded in tall trees; and last, but not least, at the famous Leek Hotel, where ruleth Mrs Lewis, great and wise, over the four months' Babylon of guides, cars, chambermaids, tourists, artists, and reading-parties, camp-stools, telescopes, poetry-books, blue uglies, red petticoats, and parasols of every hue.

# Llanystumdwy

## *Thomas De Quincey (1785-1859)*

*In the book de Quincey recalls his escape from the unhappiness of his school in Manchester in 1802, when he was seventeen.*
*He subsequently spent a rather precarious period in North Wales.*

### *From "Confessions of an English Opium Eater"*

From the keen appetite produced by constant exercise and mountain air, acting on a youthful stomach, I soon began to suffer greatly on this slender regimen; for the single meal which I could venture to order was coffee or tea. Even this, however, was at length withdrawn; and afterwards, so long as I remained in Wales, I subsisted either on blackberries, hips, haws, etc., or on the casual hospitalities which I now and then received, in return for such little services as I had an opportunity of rendering. Sometimes I wrote letters of business for cottagers, who happened to have relatives in Liverpool or in London; more often I wrote love-letters to their sweethearts for young women who had lives as servants in Shrewsbury, or other towns on the English border. On all such occasions I gave great satisfaction to my humble friends, and was generally treated with hospitality; and once in particular, near the village of Llan-y-styndw (or some such name), in a sequestered part of Merionethshire, I was entertained for upwards of three days by a family of young people, with an affectionate and fraternal kindness that left an impression upon my heart not yet impaired. The family consisted, at that time, of four sisters and three brothers, all grown up, and all remarkable for elegance and delicacy of manners. So much beauty, and so much native good-breeding and refinement, I do not remember to have seen before or since in any cottage, except once or twice in Westmoreland and Devonshire. They spoke English, an accomplishment not often met with in so many members of one family, especially in villages remote from the high-road. Here I wrote, on my first introduction, a letter about prize-money, for one of the brothers, who had served on board an English man-of-war; and more privately, two love-letters for two of the sisters. They were both interesting looking girls, and one of uncommon loveliness. In the midst of their confusion and blushes, whilst dictating, or rather giving me general instructions, it did not require any great penetration to discover that what they wished was that their letters should be as kind as was consistent with proper maidenly pride. I contrived so to temper my expressions, as to reconcile the gratification of both feelings; and they were as much pleased with the way in which I had expressed their thoughts, as (in their simplicity) they were astonished at my having so readily discovered them. The reception one meets with from the women of a family generally determines the tenor of one's whole entertainment. In this case I had discharged my confidential duties as secretary so much to the general satisfaction, perhaps also amusing them with my conversation, that I was pressed to stay with a cordiality which I had little inclination to resist. I slept with the brothers, the only unoccupied bed standing in the apartment of the young women; but in all other points they treated me with a respect not usually paid to purses as light as mine — as if my scholarship were sufficient evidence that I was of "gentle blood". Thus I lived with them for three days, and great part of a fourth; and, from the undiminished kindness which they continued to show me, I believe I might have stayed with them up to this time, if their power had corresponded with their wishes. On the last morning, however, I perceived upon their countenances, as they sat at breakfast, the expression of some unpleasant communication which was at hand; and soon after one of the brothers explained to me that their parents had gone, the day before my arrival, to an annual meeting of Methodists, held at Caernarvon, and were that day expected to return; "and if they should not be so civil as they ought to be," he begged, on the part of all the young people, that I would not take it amiss. The parents returned, with churlish faces, and *"Dym Sassenach"* *(no English)*, in answer to all my addresses. I saw how matters stood; and so, taking an affectionate leave of my kind and interesting young hosts, I went my way. For, though they spoke warmly to their parents in my behalf, and often excused the manner of the old people, by saying it was "only their way", yet I easily understood that my talent for writing love-letters would do as little to recommend me, with two grave sexagenarian Welsh Methodists, as my Greek Sapphics or Alcaics; and what had been hospitality, when offered to me with the gracious courtesy of my young friends, would become charity when connected with the harsh demeanour of these old people. Certainly, Mr Shelley is right in his notions about old age; unless powerfully counteracted by all sorts of opposite agencies, it is a miserable corrupter and blighter to the genial charities of the human heart.

# Abererch

## A. G. Bradley (1850-1943)

*See notes under Llanrwst, Bangor, Corwen.*

### From "Highways and Byways of North Wales (1898)

The village of Abererch, lush and leafy, with its low-browed, bright-washed cottages, gay with flowery frontages, straggles along the roadside to where the sparkling Erch rushes towards its tiny estuary. The old church might well tempt you to ask where the sexton lived and call for the keys. It is worth while only if you care for local history as written on church walls and in churchyards. There are beautiful glimpses, through screens of oak leaves, of the sea, brilliant in the blue of a sunny afternoon in the full height of summer. Pastures and meadows, green as in the west of Ireland, glow between hedges laden with honeysuckle and wild roses, while white farm-houses glint through the woods and grey roofs peer above the trees. The country hereabouts is no hillier than Warwickshire, but crystal streams sing with the voice of the mountain in the hollows; and old mill wheels drone on in half-hearted fashion as if conscious that their day was all but passed. Here, too, is an ancient barn, covered with ivy or virginia creeper, standing inconsequently in the fields; there a stone wall by the roadside, a rare study in tints, and bursting out in every fissure with the bloom of heather, foxglove, gorse, and lichen and a host of humble flowers whose names do not rip so readily to the tongue. There is nothing conventional in Welsh landscape; even where the land is flat it is rarely tame. Every hundred yards brings some freshy delight of foreground, with the great mountains hanging ever and always in the sky.

# Nefyn

## Edward Thomas

*See under Beddgelert, Cader Idris, Bala.*

### From "Beautiful Wales" (1906)

There were, says the story, at a small harbour belonging to Nefyn, some houses in which several families formerly lived; the houses are there still, but nobody lives in them now. There was one family there to which a little girl belonged; they used to lose her for hours every day; so her mother was very angry with her for being so much away. "I must know," said she, "where you go for your play." The girl answered that it was to Pin-y-Wig, "The Wig Point," which means a place to the west of the Nefyn headland; it was there, she said, she played with many children. "They are very nice children, — much nicer," said the child, "than I am." "I must know whose children they are," was the reply; and one day the mother went with her little girl to see the children. It was a distance of about a quarter of a mile to Pin-y-Wig, and after climbing the slope and walking a little along the top they came in sight of the Pin. It is from this Pin that the people of Pen-yr-Allt get water, and it is from there they get it still. Now after coming near the Pin the little girl raised her hands with joy at the sight of the children. "Oh, mother," said she, "their father is with them to-day; he is not with them always; it is only sometimes that he is." The mother asked the child where she saw them. "There they are, mother, running down to the Pin, with their father sitting down." "I see nobody, my child," was the reply, and great fear came upon the mother; she took hold of the child's hand in terror, and it came to her mind at once that they were the *Tylwyth Teg.* Never afterwards was the little girl allowed to go to Pin-y-Wig: the mother had heard that the Tylwyth Teg exchanged people's children with their own.

*Penrhyn Castle*

# Bangor

## *Daniel Defoe (1660-1731)*

*See note under Conwy, Penmaenmawr, St Asaph, Holywell, Denbigh.*

### *From "A Tour through the whole island of Great Britain"*

. . . to Bangor, a town noted for its antiquity, its being a bishop's see, and an old, mean looking, and almost despicable cathedral church.

This church claims to be one of the most ancient in Britain, the people say, 'tis the most ancient; that St Daniel (to whom this church was dedicated) was first bishop here, in the year 512. They allow that the pagans, perhaps of Anglesea, ruined the church, and possessed the bishopric after it was first built, for above 100 years; nor is there any account of it from the year 512, to 1009. After this, the bishopric was ruined again by dilapidation, by one of its own bishops, whose name was Bulkeley, who, not only sold the revenues, but even the very bells, for which sacrilege he was struck blind; but this last is tradition only.

It is certainly at present a poor bishopric, and has but a poor cathedral; yet the bishops are generally allowed to hold some other good benefice *in commendam*, and the preferment seems to be a grateful introduction to the clergy, as the bishops are generally translated from hence, to a more profitable bishopric.

# Bangor

## *William Graeme Tomkins*

*Tomkins Journals remain unpublished and are deposited with Clwyd Records Office. See also under Holywell.*

### *From his Journals: 1834*

An old gentleman and an old lady kindly offered to us admission to Penrhyn Castle which they had procured. We thanked them and, having secured a seat in the car from the house, journeyed very pleasantly. The castle is the residence of Mrs Pennant, the great slate quarry proprietor, and along the road the fences and walls even show signs of this source of wealth. The house itself is quite a modern structure and exceedingly extensive though we were afraid it was not half finished. Its' site was the same as the castle from which it attains the name and Mrs Pennant in her truly laudible style has determined to use nothing but British material in a British castle.

# Bangor

## *A. G. Bradley (1850-1943)*

*See note under Llanrwst, Abererch, Corwen.*

### *From "The Highways and Byways of North Wales (1898)*

A great deal beyond a doubt could be said of Bangor. But when one has travelled for twenty miles along such a road as this, and finds oneself face to face with a cathedral and University town of ten thousand souls, and all our space frittered away, rightly or wrongly, among scenes that seem to take our fancy more, what is there to be done? There is nothing indeed worthy of much remark in the winding, narrow streets, which mostly tend towards the cathedral precincts, and do not seem to have altered within my memory, though at the opening of the century there were not two thousand people in the place. Bangor Cathedral is, of all British cathedrals, held in least repute, as an edifice that is to say. For if, as I ventured to remark at St. Asaph, we choose to think of something else than architecture, there is no end to the thoughts which its stones and site and precincts, and, indeed, so venerable a building, may awaken. St. Deiniol founded it in the 6th century, and became its first abbot. The Saxon Harold gutted it, in part at any rate. Owen Glyndwr burnt it wholly down; Owen Gwynedd lies buried beneath it. But to talk about what has been done on this time-honoured spot, would be to write the history of Wales.

Students in cap and gown streaming up and down the street, or loitering round the old Cathedral yard, give a touch of academic distinction to Bangor, and remind us that one of the three colleges that form the University of Wales is here.

Bangor cherishes with much fervour that spirit of rivalry towards its sister towns that is so notable in Wales. The national aspirations find in the very spirit of localism that feeds them a serious drag upon their flights. Whether it is a football match (for the towns, I need not say, are in this respect emancipated), or an Eisteddfod, or a new college, an amount of heat is introduced that would astonish the phlegmatic Saxon. There are, for example, three colleges and three bodies of professors in little Wales, at Bangor, Cardiff and Aberystwyth, with all the waste and weakness one may fairly presume this must imply, because every town of note would have the new University within their own bounds or nowhere.

# Anglesey

## *Gerald of Wales — Geraldus Cambrensis (1146-1223)*

*From Gerald, born at Manobier in South Pembrokeshire, we have two of the earliest accounts of Wales and the Welsh people.*
*In 1188 he accompanied Archbishop Baldwin of Canterbury on a journey to secure support for the third Crusade, and the Latin texts "Hinerararium Kambriae" and "Descriptio Kambriae" were written as a result. Gerald's own ecclesiastical career was*

*cut short by hostility from the English crown: he was twice nominated for the bishopric of*
*St. Davids, but was rejected each time.*

Close to Anglesey and almost adjoining it, there is a small island inhabited by hermits, who live in the service of God by the labour of their hands. They are remarkable in that, should they have ever quarrelled with each other for reasons of human frailty, a species of small mice, which abound on the island, consume most of their food and drink, and befoul the rest. As soon as their argument is over, the plague of mice disappears immediately. It is not to be wondered at if God's servants occasionally disagree.

The island of Anglesey is an arid stony land, rough and unattractive in appearance. It is rather like the cantref of Pebidiog, round St David's, to look at, but in its natural productivity it is quite different. This island produces far more grain than any other part of Wales. In the Welsh language it has always been called 'Môn Mam Cymru', which means 'Mona the Mother of Wales'. When crops have failed in all other regions, this island, from the richness of its soil and its abundant produce, has been able to supply all Wales.

On Anglesey we saw a dog which was without a tail. It had not been born that way, but had lost its tail by some accident. All the puppies which descended from it, whether through a bitch or a male dog making no difference, had the same defect from birth.

# Anglesey

## *John Milton (1608-1674)*

*Milton's well known poem "Lycidas" is dedicated to the memory of a friend who was drowned in the Irish Sea in 1637.*
*What follows is a brief extract, which includes a reference to Anglesey.*

Where were ye Nymphs when the remorseless deep
Closed or'e the head of your lov'd Lycidas?
For neither were ye playing on the steep,
Where your old Bards, the famous Druids lie,
Nor on the shaggy top of Mona high,
Nor yet where Deva spreads her wisard stream;
Ay me, I fondly dream!

*South Stack, Holyhead*

Had ye been there for what could that have done?
What could the Muse her self that Orpheus bore,
The Muse her self, for her enchanting son
Whom universal nature did lament,
When by the rout that made the hideous roar,
His goary visage down the stream was sent,
Down the swift Hebrus to the Lesbian shore.

# Anglesey

## *Jonathan Swift (1667-1745)*

*Swift, although born in Dublin, lived much of his life in London. In the early part of the eighteenth century he made a name for himself in Londons' political and literary circles. But with the fall of the Tory ministry, of which he was a strong support, he returned to He was disliked by many, and the black mood of this extract reflects his feelings while vehement satire "Gullivers' Travels".*

*He was disliked by many and the black mood of this extract reflects his feelings while awaiting a sailing to Ireland.*

### From "Ode to Holyhead"

Lo here I sit at Holy Head
With muddy ale and mouldy bread;
All Christian vittles stink of fish;
I'm where my enemies would wish.
Convict of lies is every sign
The inn has not one drop of wine.
I'm fastened both by wind and tide,
I see the ship at anchor ride.
The captain swears the sea's too rough
He had not passengers enough
And thus the Dean is forced to stay.

When Mrs Welch's chimney smokes,
Tis a sign she'll keep her folks,
When of smoke the room is clear
It is a sign we shan't stay here.


# Anglesey

## *Rev. G. J. Freeman*

### *From "Sketches in Wales" (1826)*

On arriving at Holyhead, I chose to go to Mr Moran's Hotel, where we immediately deposited our coats and luggage, and ordered breakfast. But while this was preparing, we followed, and mixed with the long and motley train that were hastening to the pier, where we witnessed the embarkation of the mail bags and passengers, on board Captain Powers' steam-packet, for Ireland. This was a gratification of a novel kind. Captain P. himself afforded us some amusement. That gentleman had the appearance of a right merry fellow when he pleased, but never without recollections of office. His air was authoritative, his voice loud and quick, and his orders were obeyed on board and ashore, as though they were the fiat of destiny. He moved his chapeau to all strangers who were well-dressed, and familiarly shook hands with old acquaintance. Exactly at half past six, he sung out, with watch in hand, "Is all a-board?" and receiving affirmative reply, he ordered the vessel to be shoved off. Three of the hands immediately stepped forward, and applying their arms and bodies to the masonry of the pier, the packet was disengaged, and the steam-engine being set in motion, the vessel darted forward with rapidity, and soon cleared the pier head. Its movement struck me as harsh lines in a picture would do. I revolted from it as unnatural; but this was only because I was unaccustomed to it. With all its celerity of motion, there yet seemed a vast labour in the perpetual beating of the water, by the paddles of the engine; and her noise, and the stream of black smoke that came from her chimney, increased my feeling of disgust.

# Anglesey

## *Charles Dickens (1812-1870)*

*Quite apart from his fiction, Dickens wrote a tremendous number of newspaper and magazine articles. In many ways he anticipated journalism as we know it today, as he often insisted on witnessing at first hand rather than relying on second-hand information. In 1859 he visited Moelfre in order to gather material concerning the sinking of the ship The Royal Charter in October of the previous year. The vessel was returning with goods and passengers from Australia when she ran into severe difficulties. Of the five hundred passengers on board only thirty four survived. For a matter of weeks afterwards bodies were being washed ashore. Many were taken to the vicarage at Llanallgo, where the Rev Stephen Roose Hughes supervised the identification of the drowned.*
*Dickens draws largely on local accounts related to him, and information supplied by Hughes, for whom he developed a considerable admiration.*

### *From "The Uncommercial Traveller"*

We climbed towards the little church, at a cheery pace, among the loose stones, the deep mud, the wet coarse grass, the outlying water, and other obstructions from which frost and snow had lately thawed. It was a mistake (my friend was glad to tell me, on the way) to suppose that the peasantry had shown any superstitious avoidance of the drowned; on the whole, they had done very well, and had assisted readily. Ten shillings had been paid for the bringing of each body up to the church, but the way was steep, and a horse and cart (in which it was wrapped in a sheet) were necessary, and three or four men, and, all things considered, it was not a great price. The people were none the richer for the wreck, for it was the season of the herring-shoal — and who could cast nets for fish, and find dead men and women in the draught?

He had the church keys in his hand, and opened the churchyard gate, and opened the church door; and we went in.

It is a little church of great antiquity; there is reason to believe that some church has occupied the spot, these thousand years or more. The pulpit was gone, and other things usually belonging to the church were gone, owing to its living congregation having deserted it for the neighbouring school-room, and yielded it up to the dead. The very Commandments had been shouldered out of their places, in the bringing in of the dead; the black wooden tables on which they were painted, were askew, and on the stone pavement below them, and on the stone pavement all over the church, were the marks and stains where the drowned had been laid down. The eye, with little or no aid from the imagination, could yet see how the bodies had been turned, and where the head had been and where the feet. Some faded traces of the wreck of the Australian ship may be discernible on the stone pavement of this little church, hundreds of years hence, when the digging for gold in Australia shall have long and long ceased out of the land.

Forty-four shipwrecked men and women lay here at one time, awaiting burial. Here, with weeping and wailing in every room of his house, my companion worked alone for hours, solemnly surrounded by eyes that could not see him, and by lips that could not speak to him, patiently examining the tattered clothing, cutting off buttons, hair, marks from linen, anything that might lead to subsequent identification, studying faces, looking for a scar, a bent finger, a crooked toe, comparing letters sent to him with the ruin about him.

"My dearest brother had bright grey eyes and a pleasant smile," one sister wrote. O poor sister! well for you to be far from here, and keep that as your last remembrance of him!

The ladies of the clergyman's family, his wife and two sisters-in-law, came in among the bodies often. It grew to be the business of their lives to do so. Any new arrival of a bereaved woman would stimulate their pity to compare the description brought, with the dread realities. Sometimes, they would go back able to say, "I have found him," or, "I think she lies there." Perhaps, the mourner, unable to bear the sight of all that lay in the church, would be led in blindfold. Conducted to the spot with many compassionate words, and encouraged to look, she would say, with a

72

*A storm off the Anglesey coast*

piercing cry, "This is my boy!" and drop insensible on the insensible figure.

From the church, we passed out into the churchyard. Here, there lay, at that time, one hundred and forty-five bodies, that had come ashore from the wreck. He had buried them, when not identified, in graves containing four each. He had numbered each body in a register describing it, and had placed a corresponding number on each coffin, and over each grave. Identified bodies he had buried singly, in private graves, in another part of the churchyard. Several bodies had been exhumed from the graves of four, as relatives had come from a distance and seen his register; and, when recognised, these have been reburied in private graves, so that the mourners might erect separate headstones over the remains. In all such cases he had performed the funeral service a second time, and the ladies of his house had attended. There had been no offence in the poor ashes when they were brought again to the light of day; the beneficent Earth had already absorbed it. The drowned were buried in their clothes. To supply the great sudden demand for coffins, he had got all the neighbouring people handy at tools, to work the livelong day, and Sunday likewise. The coffins were neatly formed; — I had seen two, waiting for occupants, under the lee of the ruined walls of a stone hut on the beach, within call of the tent where the Christmas Feast was held. Similarly, one of the graves for four was lying open and ready, here, in the churchyard. So much of the scanty space was already devoted to the wrecked people, that the villagers had begun to express uneasy doubts whether they themselves could lie in their own ground, with their forefathers and descendants, by-and-by. The churchyard being but a step from the clergyman's dwelling-house, we crossed to the latter; the white surplice was hanging up near the door ready to be put on at any time, for a funeral service.

In this noble modesty, in this beautiful simplicity, in this serene avoidance of the least attempt to "improve" an occasion which might be supposed to have sunk of its own weight into my heart, I seemed to have happily come, in a few steps, from the churchyard with its open grave, which was the type of Death, to the Christian dwelling side by side with it, which was the type of Resurrection. I never shall think of the former, without the latter. The two will always rest side by side in my memory. If I had lost any one dear to me in this unfortunate ship, if I had made a voyage from Australia to look at the grave in the churchyard, I should go away, thankful to God that that house was so close to it, and that its shadow by day and its domestic lights by night fell upon the earth in which its Master had so tenderly laid my dear one's head.

# Anglesey

## *Francis Kilvert (1840-1879)*

*This Wiltshire-born cleric became a curate in Radnorshire and recorded his delightful impressions of people and places in his immortal Diary. It is a vivid, delicate, sometimes funny evocation of rural life in Wales during the Victorian period. In 1871 he visited North Wales.*
*See under Llangollen, Dolgellau & Cader Idris.*

### *From "The Diary"*
### *Friday 16 June, 1871*

'As we crossed the bridge (at Bangor) and were approaching the Anglesey shore we overtook a quaint humorous old man with a tall white hat, a merry twinkle in his eye, and a huge cancer in his face. I fell into talk with him. 'Now', he said as we left the Bridge and walked into Anglesey, 'now you are like Robinson Crusoe, you are on your island. How should you like to live in that house all the year round, winter and summer?' he said pointing to a white house on a little rock island in the straits. I said I thought there might be worse places. 'They live like fighting cocks there', winked the old man with the merry twinkle in his eye and his tall white hat nodding from side to side. 'They have got a weir there and they catch all the fish.'

# Harlech

## *Joseph Hucks (1772-1800)*

*Hucks undertook his tour of the region in 1794, when he was a Cambridge graduate. He was accompanied by the poet Coleridge, at that time a fellow student. Their seperate impressions of this excursion make very interesting reading.*
*See under The Dee, Dolgellau and Cader Idris.*

### *From "A Pedestrian Tour of North Wales" (1794)*

It was with much difficulty that we found our way to Harlech. We made some enquiries at a small village, but in vain; for though we addressed ourselves to many, we could by no means make them understand us; all we received in return was a stare, immediately followed by a grin, and concluded with a 'dim sarcenick', which signifies 'no Saxon'. We were obliged therefore to rely upon chance for our guide, which did not however upon this occasion befriend us; for, instead of keeping to the right upon the hills, we pursued the left path that brought us into an extensive vale, or marsh, where, at the distance of about five miles we first perceived the objects we were in pursuit of (viz). the town and castle of Harlech. After some considerable exertions, we were obliged to abandon this valley because it was so swampy, and so much intersected by ditches and drains that it would have been, if not impracticable, at least extremely uncomfortable and difficult to proceed. With great fatigue and perseverance we climbed up the almost perpendicular and craggy sides of the mountain which bounded that part of the vale and at length reached Harlech; for the first time heartily fatigued.

The country people have no idea that a stranger can be ignorant of their roads; we have not unfrequently asked the way and received for answer 'that it was as straight as we could go'; when, in a very few places, we have been perplexed by two roads, one declining to the right, and the other to the left. Nor have they much idea of distance, each measuring it by the rule of his own judgment and opinion. It is no unusual thing to be told that the distance to such a place may be about five miles, 'and a pretty good step'; which pretty good step generally proves to be about five miles more.

# Harlech

## *H. V. Morton (1892-1979)*

*H. V. Morton was born at Asthon-under-Lyme and worked as a journalist for many years. However he gave this up eventually in order to concentrate on travel writing. "In search of Wales" is one of a series of books about various countries which all have the title prefix "In Search Of . . . "*
*See also under Barmouth, Rhyl, Colwyn bay.*

### *From "In Search of Wales" (1932)*

If you asked me to pick one view which sums up Wales, I would take you to a high wall above the sea and ask you to look north to Snowdon.

This view seems to me as Welsh as the cliffs of Dover are English, as the Valley of the Tweed is Scottish, and as the Kerry Hills are Irish: it is one of those unforgettable landscapes which print themselves for ever on the mind; it is a memory of home which must have pained and consoled countless Welshmen and Welshwomen in every part of the world. This is the land of the Men of Harlech . . .

A wide half-moon of bright sand sweeps in a huge curve for miles. The waves come on slowly in great semi-circles to turn over in white foam on the sand.

On the extreme right Harlech Castle rises on a stern outcrop of rock, the most defiantly placed of all Welsh castles, a ruin that might spring to life at the sound of a trumpet, a castle that seems still to remember the whistle of arrows and the movement of lances against the sky, a stronghold whose very silence seems to whisper of King Bran the Blessed, who once perched there like an eagle, and of his sister, Bronwen the White-bosomed, who became a queen in Ireland.

*Harlech Castle*

Far below is a green vale that was once the sea. The great castle faces the horizon like a knight who has fallen asleep on a hill. Miles away are the mountains of Snowdonia, hung up like a blue screen in the north.

When I looked at Harlech the mountains were in parts grape blue. Snowdon raised his head clear of cloud. The lower hills that fold themselves in long curves at his feet were a lighter blue; and away to the east and the west his companions, Moel Hebog and Moel Siabod, lifted themselves above the valleys as if cut in blue velvet.

What a view of Wales! It is the finest thing I have seen in this country! To a Welshman it must seem like a national anthem. In those blue hills the Welsh spirit hid itself, suffered, strove and survived.

'Men of Harlech in the hollow.'

Every one knows this magnificent song. It is sung every day by people who have never seen Harlech and will probably never see it.

# Cwm Bychan

## William Bingley (1774-1823)

*Bingley writes of the rocky and remote area of hill country known as Cwm Bychan, situated a few miles from Harlech. See under Snowdonia.*

### From "North Wales: Scenery, Antiquities, Customs: 1798-1801"

Conducted by Richards as my guide I went from Harlech to explore an obscure vale, about four miles distant, called Cwm Bychan, The Little Hollow.

About a mile from the town, on a large elevated moor, he pointed out to me a circle of small stones near thirty yards in diameter, with another at some distance, surrounding it. From its form and appearance I am inclined to suppose that this was one of those druidical circles in which were formerly holden the Gorfeddau, or bardic meetings . . . Cwm Bychan is a grassy dell, about half a mile in length surrounded by scenery as black and dreary as imagination can draw. On the right of its entrance there is a small pool called Llyn y Cwm Bychan, from whose edge, Carreg y Saeth, The Rock of the Arrow, (from its being the station where the ancient British sportsmen watched and killed the passing deer,) towers the blackest of all the vale. I rested myself for a while on a rock above the pool, in a situation whence I could at ease observe the rugged beauties of this romantic hollow. From hence the landscape extended in all its magnificence: the vale was seen embosomed in stupendous rocks, black and barren, and enlivened only by the patches of meagre vegetation lodged on their shelving precipices.

# Barmouth

## J. O. Halliwell

*See also under Rhyl.*

### From "Notes On Family Excursions in North Wales" (1860)

The houses are disposed in a singular and unpleasant manner on the sides of an immense sloping rock, which shelters them on the eastern side; and whole rows appear standing on the ledges, like shelves one above another;

*Barmouth*

in winding up the narrow paths among the buildings, at different stages the inhabitants may be seen standing at their doors, quietly looking over the chimneys of their neighbours. The approach is by steps cut into the rocks, the floor of one range being nearly level with that of the roof below it. There is consequently little necessity for smoking in a population so situated — the lower tier regularly regaling the one next above it with strong warm puffs, — more especially when the wind is in their favour. But the good people of Barmouth only in part follow the scriptural injunction of "building their houses on a rock," for they show, also, a predilection for the sand, and a street has been formed close to the beach. A more inconvenient place for a town can hardly be imagined; for the houses in the lower part are frequently half choked up with sand blown from the shore. One would not believe a site would be selected for a church where the yard should be filled with sand to the depth of three or four feet, and drifted against the church itself eight or ten, on one side almost blocking up the windows: yet this I saw when I was at Barmouth last year.

# Barmouth

## H. V. Morton (1892-1979)

*See notes under Harlech, Rhyl, Colwyn Bay.*

### From "In Search of Wales" (1932)

The variety and richness of the west coast of Wales, the blend of sea, marsh, mountain and woodland, makes it almost impossible to prefer one place to another. No sooner had I put down the view of Harlech with its blue screen of mountains to the north as the most perfect sight in Wales, than I found myself at Barmouth. The town, I think, has suffered, like all Welsh towns, from its architects, but on a day when the sun is bright over Barmouth and the sails of yachts move in the harbour, you might be looking at some smaller, less exotic Gibraltar.

The long wooden bridge that crosses the wide Mawddach Estuary is, with Plymouth Hoe, perhaps the finest artificial promenade in Great Britain. You look inland, where the salt tide swirls and eddies, towards the mountains round Dolgelley. They lie folded against one another in long, gentle lines, flaming with gorse, green with grass, the darker belts of woodland climbing in the hollows. It is an unforgettable blend of water, mountain and wood, a view of its kind unsurpassed among the Highlands of Wales . . .

# The Mawddach Estuary

## Arthur Aikin

### From "Journal of a Tour Through North Wales and Part of Shropshire" (1797)

We took leave of Dolgelley this morning, and proceeded about four miles down the river to a forge; in our way we passed Llaneltid, a flourishing village, containing several good houses, beautifully situated on the river Mawddach; it serves as a port to Dolgelley, and a good many small vessels are built here. We saw a stout brig of 168 tons on the stocks, and one of 210 tons had been launched a little before. These larger vessels, however, are unable to get out of the shallow passage from Cardigan Bay to Barmouth harbour, except by taking advantage of the equinoctial tides. At this also we met a large pleasure boat on wheels, proceeding slowly to Bala pool, for the use of Sir W. Williams Wynne. On the river side are many lime kilns, in which the hard stone lime is chiefly burnt; but in some we saw a number of cockle shells calcining, which furnish an excellent lime for manure. Proceeding still down the river, we just passed the forge, and came upon a prospect which for beauty and picturesque effect, can scarcely be equalled. The wide estuary of the Mawddach was before us, filled by the tide, and enlivened here and there by a barge or pleasure boat; the banks on each side run our alternately in steep promontories, wooded to the water's edge, so as completely to hide the termination of the river, and cause it to resemble a broad and beautiful lake; while on the south from behind the banks rose abruptly the vast and craggy cliffs that surround, and almost conceal, the summit of Cader Idris.

# Dolgellau and Cader Idris

## *William Makespeace Thackeray (1811-63)*

*This major nineteenth century novelist penned the following lines in the visitors book in an anonymous hotel in the town.*

If ever you come to Dolgellau,
Dont stop at the — Hotel,
For there's nothing to put in your belly,
And the waiter dont answer the bell.

# Dolgellau and Cader Idris

## *Joseph Hucks (1772-1800)*

*See also under The Dee, Harlech.*

### *From "A Pedestrian Tour of North Wales" (1794)*

From Barmouth to Dolgellau we were highly gratified; the road wound along a ridge of rocks, that hang over the Avonvawr, an arm of the sea;

which, at full tide, has the appearance of a large lake, surrounded with beautiful woods: The mountains on both sides, but particularly on the opposite shore, were strikingly grand; and above all, Cader Idris reared its head into the clouds, which, together with the sombre aspect of the evening, and the hollow murmurings of the sea gave an awful sublimity to the scene that cannot be described.

Dolgellau is a large and dirty town: we took up our quarters at the Golden Lion, a good hospitable inn; and next morning, after breakfast, procured a guide to conduct us to the top of Cader Idris. We armed him with stores, and warlike preparations of all kinds (to wit): ham, fowl, bread, and cheese, and brandy, and began the ascent at nine in the morning, and continued to toil for three hours and a half before we reached the top. But, alas! expectation had again flattered us; for, though it was a most lovely day in the valleys, yet here we could not see fifty yards before us; the summit of the mountain is not of greater extent than the base of a common sized room; and, on one side, falls almost perpendicularly many hundred yards in depth. When I stood upon the edge of this precipice, and looked into the frightful abyss of clouds, it put me in mind of the chaos, or void space of darkness, so finely described in Milton, when the fallen archangel stood at the gates of hell, pondering the scene before him, and viewing, with horror, the profound expanse of silence and eternal night:

. . . a dark
Illimitable ocean, without bound,
Without dimension, where length, breadth, and heighth,
And time, and place are lost.

The height of this mountain is little inferior to that of Snowdon. — The view from it, on a clear day, is grand and magnificent. Ireland, the Isle of Man, North, and South Wales, lie extended before the eye like a level map.

*Cader Idris*

# Dolgellau and Cader Idris

### *Francis Kilvert (1840-1879)*

*See under Llangollen, Anglesey.*

### *From "The Diary" — Monday, 12th June 1871*

At 1 o'clock I started with my Father for North Wales. Just before we reached Barmouth Junction the train was hailed and pulled up and a party of people came tumbling into our carriage. It was Strong, Mary and Freddy and two Misses Davies. They were staying at Barmouth and had been out into the country to visit a friend who had influence enough to hail the train as if it were an omnibus and pull it up for them. From Barmouth Junction leaving the sea we travelled up the beautiful valley to Dolgellau beside the noble estuary of the Mawddach, mountains standing close on either side of the river.

We drove to Miss Roberts' Hotel, the Golden Lion. 'Did you had your luggage?' asked the omnibus driver. I was very much struck and taken with the waitress at the Golden Lion. She said her name was Jane Williams and that her home was at Betws-y-coed. She was a beautiful girl with blue eyes, eyes singularly lovely, the sweetest saddest most weary and most patient eyes I ever saw. It seemed as if she had a great sorrow in her heart. Into the soup the cook had upset both the salt cellar and the pepper box. After dinner we went out and strolled round the town. Wombwell's menagerie had just come in and the town was all alive and swarming with people. The caravans were drawn up in the 'Marian Mawr', the marshy meadow at the back of the Hotel just outside the Golden Lion garden. It seemed so strange to hear the little children chattering Welsh. I have always had a vision of coming into a Welsh town about sunset and seeing the children playing on the bridge and this evening the dream came true.

Cader Idris is the stoniest, dreariest, most desolate mountain I was ever on. We came now to the edge of a vast gulf or chasm or bason almost entirely surrounded by black precipices rising from the waters of a small black tarn which lay in the bottom of the bason. Here the guide showed me the place at the foot of an opposite precipice where Mr Smith's body had been found. Then we stumbled and struggled on again over rough tracts and wildernesses of slate and basalt. The sun was shining on the hills below, but the mist crawled down and wrapped us as if in a shroud blotting out everything. The mists and clouds began to sweep by us in white thin ghostly sheets as if some great dread Presences and Powers were going past and we could only see the skirts of their white garments. The air grew damp and chill, the cloud broke on the mountain top and it began to rain. Now and then we could discern the black sharp peak which forms the summit looming large and dark through the cloud and rain and white wild driving mist, and it was hidden again. It is an awful place in a storm. I though of Moses on Sinai.

The rain grew heavier. The old guide could not get on very fast and told me to go on alone to the top and shelter in the hut as I could not miss the path. So I went on up the last sharp peak looming black through the dark mist and cloud, by a winding path among the great rocks and wildernesses of loose stone. For a few minutes I was alone on the top of the mountain. The thought struck me, suppose the old man should be seized with cramp in the stomach here, how in the world should I get him down or get down myself in the blinding mist? The cloud and mist and rain swept by and drove eddying round the peak. I could hear the old man chinking his iron-shod staff among the rocks and stones, as he came up the path, nearer and nearer, but till he got close to me I could not discern his white figure through the dense mist. 'This is the highest point of *Cader Idris*', he said, laying his hand upon a peak of wet living rock, *'not that'*, looking with contempt at the great conical pile of stones built upon the peak by the sappers and miners during the Ordnance Survey. He said, 'The Captain of the surveying company had his tent pitched on the top of Cader Idris for 3 summer months and never left the place. He had 18 men to wait upon him. And how many clear views do you think he got in that time?' 'Twelve', I hazarded. 'Nine', he said.

He took me down to a rude 2-roomed hut built of huge stones by his father just under the shelter of the peak, and produced for my benefit a hard-boiled egg and some slices of bread and butter. Also he gave me a woollen comforter to wrap round my neck. Then he vanished. The mist drove in white sheets and shapes past the doorless doorway and past the windows from which the window frames had been removed and the wind whistled through the chinks in the rude walls of huge stones. A large flat block of stone in the middle of the room on which I sat formed the table. It is said that if any one spends a night alone on the top of Cader Idris he will be found in the morning either dead or a madman or a poet gifted with the highest degree of inspiration.

# Dolgellau and Cader Idris

## *Edward Thomas (1878-1917)*

*Thomas writes of Cader Idris in highly romanticised terms.*
*See note under Beddgelert, Nefyn, Bala.*

### *From "Beautiful Wales"*

' . . . a range of hills stood up against the cold sky with bold lines such as a happy child will draw who has much paper and a stout crayon, and looked so that I remembered the proverb which says, that if a man goes up Cader Idris at night, by dawn he is dead, or mad, or a poet. They were immense; they filled half the sky; yet in the soft light that felt its way glimmeringly, and as if fearfully, among their vast valleys and along their high crags, they looked like ruins of something far more mighty; the fields also, on this side of them, and all the elder-loving streams, and mossy woods, were but as the embers of something which the night had made and had only half destroyed before its flight. And it was with surprise that, as I took my eyes off the prospect and looked down and in the hedge, I saw that I was in a place where lotus and agrimony and vetch were yellow and the wild rose continued as ever to hesitate between red and white.'

# Corris

## *M. Vivian Hughes*

*Vivian Hughes is the author of three delightful autobiographical works, "A London Child of the Seventies", "A London Girl of the Eighties", and "A London Home In The Nineties".*
*Her evocation of middle class English life in the Victorian era is superb, and it is perhaps surprising that her books are not more widely known.*
*As a girl she spent holiday periods in North West Wales, and here she writes of life in the remote community of Corris.*

### *From "A London Girl in the Eighties"*

I hardly wonder at a country parson's taking to drink. Often enough he is sufficiently educated to be dissatisfied with the mental capacity of his flock, but not sufficiently to content himself with books or a hobby. It was so in Corris. There the little church that serves the whole district stands in the loveliest surroundings. Thither, twice every Sunday, the whole Hughes family walked the long way from Aberllefeni. Mr Hughes, as a churchwarden, sat in a front pew, with his wife and boys in a solid phalanx. Arthur had a vivid recollection of Alfred's trying to play with a hassock once, and being taken out then and there and whipped in the churchyard. A little later Alfred was to figure in another scene; one Sunday morning the whole neighbourhood was duly mustered, but no parson. People began to look about them and whisper their wonder. The situation became tense. At last, by consultations and urgent gestures Mr Hughes was induced to go over the vicarage to see what was the matter (although the congregation had little doubt as to its nature). If any one could manage a difficulty, he could. Another wait, more hopeful, but still rather too long. Mrs Hughes then took a hand (knowing her husband). As Alfred was sitting at the end of the pew she leant over to him and told him

86

to run to the vicarage and bring his father back, whatever. Again a long wait. I had this story from Alfred himself, and how he laughed at the recollection of that errand. As he came up to the vicarage he saw the old housekeeper standing at the door, looking very agitated.

"Come in, come in, my little boy,' she cried, obviously relieved that somebody had appeared in her trouble, and showed Alfred into the study. There sat his father and the vicar, both comfortably drinking, but too far gone to move.

Of crime in the valley there seemed to be none. Once only did the well-known policeman, who patrolled the whole district, appear at Mrs Hughes's door. Some days previously a disreputable-looking tramp had come to her and begged for an old coat. She searched the house, but all she could find, that was not actually in use, was a richly embroidered waistcoat that her father had worn years ago at some civic function in Shrewsbury. Why keep things just for sentiment, thought she, and gave it to the tramp. It was an embarrassing gift, for if displayed it took away the look of poverty that was his chief asset. So he stripped and wore it next his skin until he should find a possible market for it. However, at his next casual home he was required to have a bath, and the waistcoat was discovered. 'Mrs Hughes of Fronwen gave it to me', he asserted. The idea of such a gift to a tramp was so ridiculous that the policeman had come all the way to have the story confirmed, but he might have guessed that no tramp in his senses would steal such an unnegotiable thing.

# Bala

## *John Byng*

*Byng was born into a naval family and was the grandson of a viscount. During the Seven Year War he served in the Army and when peace was resumed took a senior post with the Inland Revenue at Somerset House. In 1784 he payed a fairly brief visit to North Wales.*

### *From "Tours through England and Wales between 1781 and 1794"*

Bala is a mean market town, the houses low, black, and shabby; the inhabitants, who seem very poor, have a small manufactory of stockings, and are not much accustom'd to eat wheaten bread. I should suppose that Bala must bear a flattering resemblance to some of the better sort of towns in Scotland. In the evening, we stroll'd about, and sat for some time, on a rais'd mount, (probably, old castle ground), to enjoy the bewitching prospect; then return'd to tea; and, at 6 o'clock, 'Our Galley down the silver Bala row'd', equip'd with a quantity of fishing tackle, and able steersmen. This is the poetical description. But the truth was, that we were rowled about in a little leeky boat, paddled by a plaisterer; that we had 2 bad rods with miserable lines; and that, at the end of two hours, we caught one little fish; when we landed, and walk'd on the banks of this beautiful water, till night overtook us. The lake belongs to Sr W. W. Wynn, who has for certain reasons, (unaccountable), taken away the swans, one of its beauties; which is a loss that even money cannot easily replace: the depth, in some places, is 20 fathoms, and it abounds with trout and perch, and a fresh water whiting peculiar to the place: perch sells at 2d., and trout at 3d. the pd.

In winter there is a variety of shooting, on, and around it; during the last, numbers of ducks were caught frozen to the surface; and tho it was a sheet of ice, yet there were no skaiters. These were the accounts of our boatman; who added, that harping, and dancing, were decreasing in Wales, by the interdiction of the Methodists, who over-run the country.

# Bala

## *Samuel Taylor Coleridge (1772-1834)*

*While accompanying his friend Joseph Hucks on a tour of North Wales in 1794 Coleridge, writing to his friend Robert Southey described a heated political argument at an inn in Bala.*
*See under Abergele, Denbigh, Llangollen.*

Shortly after, into the same room a well drest clergyman and four others — among whom (the Landlady whispers me) was a Justice of Peace and the Doctor of the Parish — I was asked for a Gentleman (i.e. to propose a toast) — I gave General Washington. The parson said in a low voice — Republicans!) — After which the medical man said — damn Toasts! I gives a sentiment — May all Republicans be *gulloteen'd!* — Up starts the Welch Democrat — May all *Fools* be gulloteen'd — and then you will be the first! Thereon Rogue, Villain, Traitor flew thick in each other's faces as a hailstorm — This is nothing in Wales — they *make calling one another*

*Llyn Tegid, near Bala*

*Liars &'c* — necessary vent-holes to the sulphurous Fumes of the Temper!
At last, I endeavored to arbitrate by observing that whatever might be our
opinions in politics, the appearance of a Clergyman in the Company
assured me, we were all *Christians* — tho' (continued I) it is rather difficult
to reconcile the last Sentiment with the Spirit of Christianity. Pho! —
quoth the Parsòn — Christianity! Why, we an't at Church now? Are we?
— The Gemman's Sentiment was a very good one — 'it shewed, he was
*sincere* in his principles! ['] ) Welsh Politics could not prevail over Welch
Hospitality — they all except the Parson shook me by the hand, and said I
was an open hearted honest-speaking Fellow, tho' I was a bit of a
Democrat.

# Bala

## *Edward Thomas (1878-1917)*

*See notes under Beddgelert, Nefyn, Dolgellau & Cader Idris.*

### *From "Beautiful Wales"*

There is a tradition that Bala Lake covers old palaces. It is said that they have been seen on clear moonlit nights, when the air is one sapphire, and that a voice is heard saying, "Vengeance will come", and another voice, "When will it come?" and again the first voice saying "In the third generation". For a prince once had a palace where the lake is. He was cruel and persisted in his cruelty, despite a voice that sometimes cried to him, "Vengeance will come". One night there was a bright festival at the palace, and there were many ladies and many lords among the guests, for an heir had just been born to the prince. The wine shone and was continually renewed. The dancers were merry and never tired. And a voice cried "Vengeance". But only the harpist heard; and he saw a bird beckoning him out of the palace. He followed, and if he stopped, the bird called "Vengeance". So they travelled a long way, and at last he stopped and rested, and the bird was silent. Then the harper upbraided himself, and turned and would have gone back to the palace. But he lost his way, for it was night. And in the morning he saw one calm large lake where the palace had been; and on the lake floated the harpers harp.

# CLWYD

## Hawarden

### *Louisa Costello*

*In the passage below we are reminded of the spread of industrialism in the region in the first half of the nineteenth century.*
*See under Maentwrog.*

#### *From "The Falls, Lakes and Mountains of North Wales" (1839)*

Hawarden Castle is a fine ruin, on an eminence above the modern dwelling, in the charming park of Sir Stephen Glynne, where the lawns and graceful hills covered with luxuriant trees are extremely inviting. We wandered about there on a warm summer day in uninterrupted solitude, and enjoyed the fine view from the broken towers, festooned with shining ivy: nothing disturbed the stillness but the murmuring of the numerous bees, which seemed to delight in the warm spot, and who for a time forsook the rich gardens of roses which had attracted them below. Presently, however, we heard a low booming sound, which we mistook for the organ of the distant church; but on descending from the castle height our romance was dispelled, by finding that it was the noise of an iron foundry, so close to the gardens that the smoke sweeps over them, and greatly destroys the effect we had been admiring.

## Flint

### *Celia Fiennes (1662-1741)*

*Celia Fiennes (pronounced Fines) was a remarkable woman. She was the daughter of a Cromwellian colonel, and at an early age developed considerable independence of thought. Most of what we know about her is derived from her Journal, of which an incomplete version appeared in 1888. She rode through every English County describing what she saw in her own interesting manner over a period of years.*
*Despite the fact that Celia Fiennes' travels were mainly in England, she did come over the border into Flintshire briefly.*
*See under Holywell.*

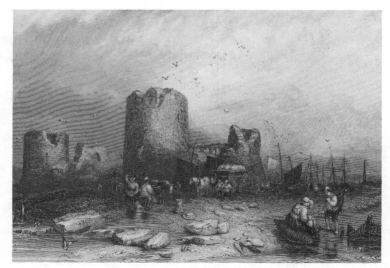

*Flint castle*

### From "The Journeys of Celia Fiennes"

' . . . pass'd thro' Flint town; its a very ragged place . . . the houses all thatched and stone walls but so decay'd that in many places ready to tumble down; there was a town wall such a one as it was; it was a Session tyme when I was there which shew'd it at its prime; there is a castle which still remains . . . '

# Holywell

### Celia Fiennes (1662-1741)

*See under Flint.*

### From "The Journeys of Celia Fiennes"

' . . . it seems the Saint they do honour to in this place must beare them out in all things, they tell of many lameness's and aches and distempers which are cured by it; its a cold water and cleare and runs off very quick so that it would be pleasant refreshment in the summer to washe onesself in it, but its shallow not up to the waist so its not easy to dive and washe in . . . I saw abundance of the devout papists on their knees all round the wall; poor people are deluded into an ignorant blind zeale and to be pity'd by us that have the advantage of knowing better and ought to be better; there is some small stones of a reddish coullour in the well said to be some of St Winifred's blood also, which the poor people take out and bring to the strangers for curiousity and relicts, and also moss about the bancks full of great virtue for every thing — but its a certain game to the poore people, every one gives them something for bringing them moss and the stones . . . '

'At Holly Well they speake Welsh, the inhabitants go barefoote and bare leg'd a nasty sort of people, their meate is very small here, the mutton is noe bigger than little lamb, and what of it is very sweete; their wine good being near the sea side and are all well provided with fish.'

# Holywell

## Daniel Defoe (1660-1731)

*See notes under Conwy, Snowdonia, Bangor, St Asaph, The Vale of Clwyd, Penmaenmawr.*

### From "A Tour Through The Whole Island of Great Britain"

. . . we came to Holly-well. The stories of this Well of S. Winifrid are, that the pious virgin, being ravished and murthered, this healing water sprung out of her body when buried; but this smells too much of the legend, to take up any of my time; the Romanists indeed believe it, as 'tis evident, from their thronging hither to receive the healing sanative virtue of the water, which they do not hope for as it is a medicinal water, but as it is a miraculous water, and heals them by virtue of the intercession and influence of this famous virgin, St Winifrid; of which I believe as much as comes to my share.

# Holywell

## *Richard Warner (1763-1857)*

*See notes under Conwy, Abergele, Snowdonia.*

### *From "A Second Walk Through Wales"*

Its wonder-working well rendered it a place of notoriety in former times, and its numerous manufactories and valuable mines stamp it with much more real importance in the present day. Of local customs there is nothing particular, (since the resort of Roman Catholics to the well has ceased) except an unusual mode of summoning the inhabitants to church. This edifice is so situated, that when the wind blows from the south or the south-west, the bell cannot be heard in most parts of the town; the parishioners, therefore, allow an annual stipend to a poor man, to notify the hour of prayer on Sundays and Holidays, which he does in the following singular manner: — A leathern strap is suspended round his neck, and a large and heavy bell attached to it, which rests upon a cushion buckled over his knee. Thus accoutred, he traverses the town, jingling his bell, to the surprise of those who are unacquainted with the custom. A ridiculous circumstance happened in consequence of this practice a short time since; an honest Hibernian, who, in passing through Holywell, sojourned there a day to see its curiosities, was standing at the door of the inn when this ecclesiastical bellman paraded the streets in the exercise of his office. The traveller, astonished at the sight, enquired of a fellow standing by, who had more shrewdness than good-nature, the cause of it, and received for answer that it was to announce the arrival of an *oyster-boat* at the *well*. The credulous Milesian, who was very partial to this shell-fish, instantly hurried thither, in order to make a first purchase; but found to his confusion, on enquiring for the vessel, that it was utterly impossible, from the situation of the place, any sort of boat should approach within a mile of it — a disappointment that was rendered still more painful, by the gibes and jeerings of the female attendants at the well. Foaming with rage, he returned to the inn, resolved to repay the trick that had been exercised upon him, with his faithful *shilalah*; but here again he reckoned without his host, for the wit, satisfied with the success of the first part of the joke, and not chusing to wait the conclusion of it, had retired from the inn to tell the tale of cheated simplicity.

*St Winifred's Well, Holywell*

# Holywell

## *William Graeme Tompkins*

*See under Bangor.*

### *From his "Journals" (1834)*

Basingwerk Abbey is very extensive and very beautiful. Our guide gave some vague and unspecified account of some battle having been fought there, but could not say when. On being asked whether it was at the time of Cromwell he said yes he thought it was. He pointed out an oak, very old and shaggy, and said several of the bullets were embedded, one of which I extracted.

# The Dee

## *Joseph Hucks (1772-1800)*

*See under Dolgellau & Cader Idris, The Vale of Clwyd, Harlech.*

### *From "A Pedestrian Tour of North Wales" (1794)*

About three miles on this side of Holywell, there is a very extensive prospect. From the summit of a hill, we commanded a view of the Dee, incorporating its waters with the ocean. Far beyond, though considerably involved in a thick smoke, appeared Liverpool, the seat of busy commerce; and to the right, Park-gate, a favourite watering place, the abode of pleasure, and of song. I could not help smiling at the present appearance of the river Dee, compared with what it was when I formerly beheld it; at that time unconscious of its future greatness, it murmured over its craggy bed, or smoothly glided through the meadows and rich pastures, where numerous herds of cattle were feeding, or seeking to allay the sultry heat, in the midst of the stream. Many humble cottages rose upon its banks, presenting interesting pictures of content and happiness; children busily employed in picking sloes from the bushes that hung over the stream, or amusing themselves with throwing pebbles into the water, thus sporting with time, and 'reckless that age and sorrow with icy hand hung over them.'

# The Dee

## *Charles Kingsley (1819-1875)*

*See also under Snowdonia, Porthmadog.*

### *The Sands of Dee*

'O Mary, go and call the cattle home,
  And call the cattle home,
  And call the cattle home,
  Across the sands of Dee.'
The western wind was wild and dark with foam,
  And all alone went she.

The western tide crept up along the sand,
    And o'er and o'er the hand,
    And round and round the sand,
    As far as eye could see.
The rolling mist came down and hid the land:
    And never home came she.

'O is it weed or fish or floating hair —
    A tress of golden hair,
    A drowned maiden's hair,
    Above the nets at sea?'
Was never salmon yet that shone so fair
    Among the stakes of Dee.

They row'd her in across the rolling foam,
    The cruel crawling foam,
    The cruel hungry foam,
    To her grave beside the sea.
But still the boatmen hear her call the cattle home,
    Across the sands of Dee.

# The River Alun

## *Washington Irving (1783-1859)*

*This American short story writer and historian trained as a lawyer, although his natural inclination favoured a wandering life. He was also drawn to writing, and his early works quickly established his reputation.*

*His Sketch Book contains thirty-two pieces, including his two famous tales 'Rip Van Winkle' and 'The Legend of Sleepy Hollow'. Another sketch, 'The Angler' describes a visit which he made to Flintshire while serving as American consul in Liverpool. On the banks of the River Alun he encounters an aged fisherman.*

*See also under Ruthin.*

### *From "The Sketch Book"*

'In a morning stroll along the banks of the Alun, a beautiful little stream which flows down the Welsh hills and throws itself into the River Dee, my attention was attracted by a group seated on the margin. On approaching I found it to consist of a veteran angler and two rustic disciples. The former was an old fellow with a wooden leg, with clothes very well but very carefully patched, betokening poverty, honesty come by, and decently maintained . . . The day was mild and the sun shining, with now and then a soft-dropping shower that sowed the whole earth with diamonds . . . I fell into conversation with the old angler and was so much entertained that, under pretext of receiving instructions in his art, I kept company with him almost the whole day: wandering along the banks of the stream and listening to his talk . . . The whole tenor of his life was quiet and inoffensive, being principally passed about the neighbouring streams . . . at other times he employs himself at home, preparing his fishing tackle for the next campaign, or manufacturing rods, nets, and floes for his patrons and pupils among the gentry.'

On parting with the old angler I inquired after his place of abode, and happening to be in the neighbourhood of the village a few days afterwards I had the curiosity to seek him out. I found him living in an old cottage, containing only one room, but a perfect curiosity in its method and arrangement. It was on the skirts of the village, on a green bank, a little back from the road, with a small garden in front, stocked with kitchen herbs and adorned with a few flowers. The whole front of the cottage was overrun with a honeysuckle. On the top was a ship for a weathercock. The interior was filled up in a truly nautical style, his ideas of comfort and convenience having been acquired on the berth-deck of a man-of-war . . . His implements for angling were carefully disposed on nails and hooks about the room. On a shelf was arranged his library, containing a work on angling, much worn, a Bible covered with canvas, an old volume or two of voyages, a nautical almanack and a book of songs.

I found him seated on a bench before the door smoking his pipe in the soft evening sunshine. His cat was purring soberly on the threshold, and his parrot describing some strange evolutions in an iron ring, that swung in the centre of his cage. He had been angling all day, and gave me a history of his sport with as much minuteness as a general would talk over a campaign, being particularly animated in relating the manner in which he had taken a large trout, which had completely tasked all his skill and wariness, and which he had sent as a trophy to mine hostess of the inn.

# Caerwys

## *Richard Fenton*

### *From "Tours In Wales 1804-1813"*

Thursday, [Sept. 1st, 1808] — Appointed to meet Mr Roberts, the Parson of Tremeirchion, who had accompanied us yesterday at Bodfari, to continue our search and to visit Caerwys. We fell in with each other about eleven, and immediately proceeded by the same road in the Vale as we took in returning yesterday, and beyond Maes Mynnan turned to the left, a pretty sharp ascent, till we came to Caerwys, one of the Contributory Boroughs to Flint. It consists of two long ill built streets intersecting each other at right Angles, with a large Elm, surrounded by a little Bank, growing in the Centre. It is on a bed of Limestone, and therefore there is a great lack of Water, the inhabitants being obliged to send to a great distance for it, an inconvenience alone that must have prevented it from becoming a great town, which one at first sight might be tempted to suppose had been in project. They shew you a large old House which is said to have been the Town Hall, and there is a record that the Assizes were held there in the time of Charles; and there had been a person executed there, as appears by a warrant to the Sheriff, now in the Possession of Mr Pennant. There is another large old house, the greater part of which they say was the Prison.

# Rhyl

## *J. O. Halliwell*

*See also under Barmouth.*

### *From "Notes on Family Excursions in North Wales" (1860)*

A quarter of a century ago it was little more than an unenclosed common, and at first sight it seems difficult to account for the causes of its rapid progress. It has no walks, no good drives, no trees, no flowers, nothing of the picturesque, excepting the views of the mountains in the distance; it is situated on a dead flat, and moreover it is half choked with dry and flying sand; but it has beautiful air, good bathing, fine sands, and has the great advantage of cheap and easy access from Liverpool by sea. Rhyl is a chapelry in the parish of Rhuddlan. In 1811, it consisted of a few scattered dwellings, the population numbering only 252, and it was not until about the year 1828 that the place showed any symptoms of prosperity. From that time to the present it has continued in a rapid course of progress, until now it takes its place as one of the principal towns on the coast of North Wales.

When I said that there was nothing of the picturesque at Rhyl, there should have been excepted the spectacle of some of the fisherwomen, who with nets on their shoulders, blue gowns reaching to their knees, and naked feet, trudging on the sands early on a summer's morning carolling Welsh songs, — they should only have been seen on the continent by some of our sentimental travellers, and we should have had a page or two of romantic description. I can only observe that to see and hear them added a charm to the attractions of the sands of Rhyl.

# Rhyl

## Gerard Manley Hopkins (1844-1889)

*During his three year period of training for the Jesuit priesthood Hopkins became ill. He went to Rhyl in order to convalesce and while there wrote this poem. See under St Asaph, Maentwrog, The Elwy Valley, Denbigh.*

### The Sea and the Skylark

On ear and ear two noises too old to end
   Trench — right, the tide that ramps against the shore;
   With a flood or a fall, low lull-off or all roar,
Frequenting there while moon shall wear and wend.

Left hand, off land, I hear the lark ascend,
   His rash-fresh re-winded new-skeinèd score
   In crisps of curl off wild winch whirl, and pour
And pelt music, till none's to spill nor spend.

How these two shame this shallow and frail town!
   How ring right out our sordid turbid time,
Being pure! We, life's pride and cared-for crown,

Have lost that cheer and charm of earth's past prime:
Our make and making break, are breaking, down
To man's last dust, drain fast towards man's first slime.

# Rhyl

## *John Moore (1907-1967)*

*In his books John Moore presents a vivid evocation of rural life. His many works of fiction include a trilogy concerned with the village of Brensham, and he is also the author of a study of Edward Thomas.*

*His earlier works are concerned with his travels around Britain on foot and make amusing reading.*

*Moore's caustic comments on Rhyl, printed below, are to be found in "Tramping Through Wales".*

*See under Denbigh.*

### *From "Tramping Through Wales" (1931)*

In the evening, out of a sense of duty, I took a bus and went to see Rhyl.

Wild horses shall not drag from me a full account of that horror; "neither wild 'orses, nor blood 'orses, nor race 'orses, nor cart 'orses, nor Suffolk punches" — in the cumulative phrase of Mary Webb's Andrew Vesson. What I think of Rhyl is not for cold print; it belongs to flaming forbidden words which would scorch this page. But I will say this: that if one were to entrust the architecture of an important town to a committee formed from representatives of the designers of fancy cakes, dolls' houses, and toy Swiss chalets, and from the artists who paint the pictures on crackers and chocolate-box lids, with power to co-opt from the ranks of the worst jerry-builders in the country, and the worst sign-writers in the world, then the result would be a flattering imitation of the sea-front at Rhyl. The whole town resembles a cheap bazaar; indeed, its appearance of impermanence is the most pleasing thing about it. The few good buildings which it possesses seem to rise up out of a chaos of pink sugar-rock, which mocks them shamefully. Indeed, my impression of Rhyl, now six weeks old, is that it achieves an effect of staggering baroque by the admixture of bad buildings and monstrous sticks of this red and yellow stuff. But really Rhyl is indescribable; it is like the wrath of God.

*The seafront at Rhyl*

# Rhyl

## H. V. Morton (1892-1979)

*Morton was writing at approximately the same time as John Moore and his very brief comments in "In Search of Wales" make a contrast.*
*See under Harlech, Barmouth, Colwyn Bay.*

### From "In Search of Wales" (1932)

I like windy Rhyl. The tide was far out and the gold sands stretched for miles. It is one of the many seaside places in Great Britain which have grown up almost within modern times to satisfy the migratory instincts of great industrial cities.

# Rhuddlan

## Mrs Rodolph Stowell

*See under Llanrwst.*

### From "Motor Tours in Wales and the Border Counties" (1908)

' . . . as we drop down into Abergele the Morfa Rhuddlan lies before us lika a map — a dull map — with fashionable Rhyl in the distance; and from Abergele to Rhuddlan the road is surely the straightest and flattest that ever was seen.

The ivy-smothered towers of Rhuddlan Castle stand on the banks of the Clwyd. That great statesman and soldier, Edward I., being weary of the "Welsh Question," determined to get the affair finished once for all: so he rebuilt this castle, settled down here with his Court and family, conquered the country, made its laws, and saw that they were carried out. There is a remnant still standing of the house where he held his parliament and "secured its independence to the Principality of Wales." These words, though not Edward's, are quite in the spirit of his little jokes. It was here that he played his historical practical joke upon the Welsh nation, when he promised them a prince who was a native of Wales and could not speak a word of English — and then showed them the baby. There is nothing for us to see inside this castle, for Cromwell altogether dismantled it, and its heavy green towers, though impressive enough as being the grave of Welsh independence, are not nearly so typical of the "ruthless king" as his great fortresses of Carnarvon and Harlech and Conway."

# Abergele

## Richard Warner (1763-1857)

*Warner and his friends are mistaken for travelling players.*
*See under Holywell, Snowdonia, Conwy.*

### From "A Second Walk Through North Wales" (1799)

The little bathing town or Abergele afforded us some excellent London porter and Shropshire cheese. Whilst we were enjoying this repast, mine

*Rhuddlan Castle*

host, who seemed to regard our attacks upon his loaf with some astonishment, after begging pardon for making so bold, requested to know whether we were of *"the party"*. The expression was of so *Proteuslike* a nature (particularly in these days of difference and division) that we did not at all understand him, I, therefore, desired he would explain himself. "Why, gentlemen," returned he, "I wished to be informed whether you belonged to the set of *strolling players* who are lately gone to Bangor, because, if you had, I would have troubled one of you with an *old shirt* which a *gentleman of the party* left behind him instead of his reckoning, when he passed through here." We had already been taken for militia-men, plunderers, and recruits, but had no idea of the honour that awaited us, of being ranked amongst the itinerant sons of Thespis.

# Abergele

## *Rev. G. J. Freeman*

### *From "Sketches in Wales" (1826)*

At the Bee Hotel we had the gratification of finding our friends from Llangollen, all in good health and excellent spirits, and very comfortably established in a spacious room, whose windows commanded the sea. They kindly invited us to join company; in consequence of which, after having refreshed ourselves by a thorough change of linen, &c. we drew our chairs together, and had a long dish of chat upon Wales, and domestic politics, till the hour of dinner, when some fish and mutton of the best, were served up by our hostess.

Hunger having been satisfied, we were all with one accord looking towards the sea. The children, who understood the general feeling by a better language than that of the tongue, were impatient for some sign, which they might interpret into permission to put on their bonnets. The weather promising to be fair, this was readily conceded, and in a few minutes we were all bound to the sea beech, by a road which proved neither clean, even, or short. This circumstance will always be a disadvantage to Abergele as a marine resort. The distance from the village to the water's edge is full half a mile. Some of the ladies had made an excursion thither in the morning, and gave me a delightful account of the firmness and extent of the sands, so that, when arrived, I was not surprised to see a long and beautiful promenade on both sides of us as far as the eye could reach. Mr Brettell and myself had never, till this moment, stood on "the long resounding shore" together. We therefore stepped to the margin of the flowing tide and *shook hands*, a wonted custom with us upon anything highly gratifying.

# Abergele

## *Samuel Taylor Coleridge (1771-1834)*

*See under Bala, Llangollen, Denbigh.*

Abergele is a large village on the sea coast. Walking on the sea sands I was surprised to see a number of fine women bathing promiscuously with men and boys perfectly naked! Doubtless, the citadels of their chastity are so impregnably strong that they need not the ornamental outworks of modesty. But seriously speaking, where sexual distinctions are least observed men and women live together in the greatest purity. Concealment sets the imagination a working . . . Just before I quitted Cambridge I met a countryman with a strange walking stick, five feet in length. I eagerly bought it and a most faithful servant it has proved to be. My sudden affection for it has mellowed into settled friendship. On the morning of our leaving Abergele just before our final departure I looked for the stick in the place where I had left it overnight. It was gone! I alarmed the house. No one knew anything of it. In the flurry of anxiety I sent for the crier of the town and gave him the following to cry about the town and on the beach, which he did with a gravity for which I am indebted to his stupidity.

'Missing form the Bee Inn, Abergele, a curious walking stick. On one side it displays the head of an eagle . . . On the other side is the portrait of the owner in wood work . . . If any gentleman or lady has fallen in love with the above described stick and secretly carried it off, he or she is hearby earnestly admonished to conquer a passion, the contiuance of which must prove fatal to his or her honesty; and if the said stick has slipped into such gentlemans or ladies hands through inadvertence, he, or she, is required to rectify the mistake with all convenient speed. God save the King.'

Abergele is a fashionable Welsh watering place and so singular a proclamation excited no small crowd on the beach, among the rest a lame old gentleman in whose hands I espied my stick. The old gent, who lodged at our inn, felt great confusion, and walked homeward, the solemn crier before him, and a various cavalcade behind . . . He made his lameness an apology for borrowing my stick . . . Thus it ended . . .

# Colwyn Bay

## H. V. Morton (1892-1979)

*See note under Harlech, Barmouth, Rhyl.*

### From "In Search of Wales" (1932)

It is not difficult to see why Colwyn Bay has become one of the most popular places in North Wales. Gold sands, a great half circle of sea, hills, woods and streams. The semi circle of hills on the south and west give to this place what doctors call a 'local climate'. Like all these northern watering places in Wales a large part of their popularity is due to the fact that you can be tucked away in the town, but half an hour's walking takes you to hills and winds from the Atlantic.


# The Vale of Clwyd

## Michael Drayton (1563-1631)

*Michael Drayton, who was born in Warwickshire, is probably best remembered as the author of "Polyalbion" (1622), a topographical poem which has much antiquarian and historical detail.*
*In the following section he writes of the Vale of Clwyd.*

### From "Polyablion"

The North-wind (calme become) forgets his Ire to wreake,
And the delicious Vale thus mildly doth bespeake;
Deere *Cluyd*, th'aboundant sweets, that from thy bosome flowe,
When with my active wings into the ayre I throwe,
Those Hills whose hoarie heads seeme in the clouds to dwell,
Of aged become young, enamor'd with the smell
Of th'odoriferous flowers in thy most precious lap:
Within whose velvit leaves, when I my selfe enwrap,
They suffocate with sents; that (from my native kind)
I seeme some slowe perfume, and not the swiftest wind.

With joy, my *Dyffren Cluyd*, I see thee bravely spred,
Survaying every part, from foote up to thy head;
Thy full and youthfull breasts, which in their meadowy pride,
Are brancht with rivery veines, Meander-like that glide.
I further note in thee, more excellent than these
(Were there a thing that more the amorous eye might please)
Thy plumpe and swelling wombe, whose mellowy gleabe doth beare
The yellow ripened sheafe, that bendeth with the eare.

# The Vale of Clwyd

## *William Camden (1551-1623)*

*Camden, historian and antiquary, became headmaster of Westminster School, where one of his pupils was Ben Jonson.*
*His compendium of British pre-history, Britannia*, appeared in Latin in 1586, and was translated into English in 1610.

The Vale of Clwyd — the heart of the county, where nature having removed the mountains on all hands hath spread out a most pleasant Vale — the complexion of the inhabitants is bright and cheerful, their heads of a sound constitution, their sight very lively, and even their old age vigorous and lasting. The green meadows, the cornfields and the numerous villages and churches afforded us the most pleasant prospect imaginable.

# The Vale of Clwyd

## *Daniel Defoe (1660-1731)*

*Here Defoe reveals his characteristic chauvinism.*
*See under Conwy, Snowdonia, Bangor, St Asaph, Penmaenmawr.*

### *From "A Tour Through The Whole Island Of Great Britain"*

This (Denbigh) is the county town, and is a large populous place, which carries something in its countenance of its neighbourhood to England, but that which was most surprising, after such a tiresome and fatiguing journey, over the unhospitable mountains of Merioneth, and

Carnarvonshire, was, that descending now from the hills, we came into a most pleasant, fruitful, populous, and delicious vale, full of villages and towns, the fields shining with corn, just ready for the reapers, the meadows green and flowery, and a fine river, with a mild and gentle stream running through it: nor is it a small or casual intermission, but we had a prospect of the country open before us, for above 20 miles in length, and from 5 to 7 miles in breadth, all smiling with the same kind of complexion; which made us think our selves in England again, all on a sudden.

# The Vale of Clwyd

## *Joseph Hucks (1772-1800)*

*See under Dolgellau & Cader Idris, The Dee, Harlech.*

### *From "A Pedestrian Tour Of North Wales" (1794)*

. . . the vale of Clwyd, in all its beauty, unfolded upon the sight: it appeared like a moving picture, upon which nature had been prodigal of its colours. Hamlets, villages, towns, and castles, rose like enchantment upon this rich carpet, that seemed covered with wood and enclosures; in the midst of it, at the distance of about five miles, the town of Ruthin, partially appeared from the bosom of a most beautiful grove of trees; the vale on each side being bounded by a chain of lofty mountains, and far off, on a bold and rugged promontory, stood Denbigh, with its strong fortress, the undisputed mistress of this extended scene.

# The Vale of Clwyd

*Late nineteenth century Denbighshire became a whirlpool of political and religious activity.*

*Thomas Gee set up a publishing house at Denbigh which was to prove very effective as a rallying point. His newspaper "Baner ac Amserau Cymru" advocated the Disestablishment of the Anglican Church in Wales, the widening of electoral sufferage, and the provision of non-sectarian education.*

### *From "Letters From Wales to 'The Times' "*
### *by a Special Correspondent: 1889*

. . . in northern Denbighshire the feeling of Welshmen upon the great questions of the day is made and created; in the town of Denbigh lives the man who wields more influence over his countrymen than any other. Moreover, northern Denbighshire, which has now become the chosen home of the Welsh National League, has been the scene of more lawless riot and disturbance than any other part of Wales. Over such a county one may well linger in the hope of discovering and appreciating the nature and the strength of the influences which have been, and still are, actively at work. Let the reader glance again at the map, or he may take my word for it if he will, and he will find that the greater part of northern Denbighshire consists of a wild tract of mountain land, which, except to the extreme west, is rarely visited by the tourist. Here the population is made up almost entirely of mountain farmers, whose fortunes vary with the rise and fall in the prices of stock in general and sheep in particular. To the eastward of this great tract lies the Vale of Clwyd, which is, from the point of view naturally taken by the writer, by far the most important part of the district. The valley runs from Rhyl in a southerly direction as far as Nantclwyd, which is some five or six miles south of Ruthin, but the visitor is not strictly in Denbighshire until he has passed St Asaph. Having travelled thus far, he finds himself, as far as appearances go, in the midst of a land of plenty. Other Welshmen say that in the Vale of Clwyd the worst of farmers thrive upon the best of land. Now, upon the first point no opinion need be expressed, since to form a judgment otherwise than superficial upon the question whether men farm well or ill were the task of years; but of the fertility of the land and of the apparent prosperity of the people there can be no question. Nowhere has it been my fortune to see a people more comfortably housed and clothed, pastures more rich or stock more thriving, than in the Vale of Clwyd. The prosperity may be apparent rather than real, the comfort of the people may be greater than their means warrant, the magnificent stock may fetch miserable prices — there is a good deal of ground, more's the pity, for all these statements, as will appear later — but there can be no shadow of a doubt that the outward signs of peace and of plenty are phenomenal.

# The Vale of Clwyd

## *Lionel Johnson (1867-1902)*

*Johnson, who was born in Kent, was associated with the Rhymers Club in the eighteen-nineties, and was much admired by Yeats.*
*He commemorated a visit to the Vale of Clwyd with a poem about Moel Fama, which is the highest of the Clwydian hills, a few miles from Ruthin.*
*His own spelling has been retained.*

### *Moel Fama*

In purple heather is my sleep
On Moel Fama; far below,
The springing rivulets leap,
The firs wave to and fro.

This morn, the sun on Bala Lake
Broke out behind me: morrow morn
Near Rhual I Shall wake,
Before the sun is born.

High burning over Clwyd vale,
And reddening the mountain dew:
While the moon lingers frail
High up in the skies of blue.

Lonely and loved, O passionate land!
Dear Celtic land, unconquered still!
Thy mountain strength prevails:
The winds have all their will.

They have no care of meaner things;
They have no scorn for brooding dreams:
A spirit in them sings,
A light about them beams.

*Town Hall, Ruthin*

# Ruthin

## *Wilfred Owen (1893-1918)*

*One of the finest poets of his generation.*
*Wilfred Owen was born in Oswestry, and grew up in Birkenhead. He served in the First World War, but was killed shortly before the Armistice. Of his work he said, "the subject of it is War and the pity of War".*
*In 1905 the young Wilfred went on holiday with a friend Alec Paton. They stayed at a farm which was owned by an aunt and uncle of Alec's at the village of Rhewl, near Ruthin. While there Wilfred wrote delightful letters home to his mother.*

Glan Clwyd,
Rhewl.
Aug. 7th 1905.

Dear Mother,

   Thank you very much for the boots, which I received this morning. It has been so wet here that I changed my shoes and stockings 3 times on Saturday and Alec & I put our feet in hot water when we went to bed. Our feet were only just a little damp, & Mr Paton laughed & said they were all right, but Mrs Paton made us change. (Don't tell any one this!) At first, before we got to the farm the place was not what I anticipated, we had to go *through*, not along, a dirty, wet, muddy lane. But the farm is fine. I am very happy but I am not wild. We are both kept under great restriction. We got up a ladder on to a hay-stack in a Dutch Barn. In case you don't know what a D.B. is, I will draw one.

Well, we made little nests on the top but Mrs Paton heard us moving the hay & soon called us down. (Mr P. laughed). I am asked to thank Mr Owen for the f.rod. It is useless now! We cannot fish!! No lisence!!! Is it not sad!!! Alec's Uncle broke my rod, it is mended now. He was fishing this morning when a river bailiff came up and told him something about how to fish, thinking he had a lisence! You have to pay 15 or 16 shillings for 1 to fish I *think*. This is a filthy letter, all blots. Thank Mary and Colin for their letters. I slept in chair bed 1st night but I do not now I sleep with Alec.

From your loving

Wilfred.

Aug. 16. 1905.

Dear Mother

I am so sorry you were not well on Sunday. I thought about you very often, nearly all day. We climbed Moel Fama (Varma) on the 14th. I was rather exhausted by the time we reached the top. It was about 4 o'clock, started at 11.30, but when we got home I was hardly so bad as the others were. Alec made a show of sliding down the smooth slippery grass, but he found he could not stop himself. He went bounding on till he was suddenly checked by a sharp stone wall. We thought he had hurt his head, but he had a deep cut on the knee, he said he was able to climb the hill though! I was lying down at the time, resting. Thank you very much for the letter & Turkish Delight. I have had a little bad luck. Up Moel Fama I lost my big fat knife I think. I am very sorry to say I broke the end of your umbrella. We tried to fish with the end of our rods in a tiny stream that runs into the Clwyd. I lent Alec a hook which he lost, & I lost my own, & cracked the tip end of my rod. I have bought a Picture Postcard for Harold which I hope to send tomorrow.

With best love to all<br>From<br>Wilfred.

Dear Mother

I hope you are all quite well I am eating tremendously. We went gathering nuts this morning I have got, altogether, 113. I am going to bring them home for the children you must not tell them please. Mr Jones has bought 120 sheep today. They are so tired after walking three days that some will let me stroke them. I can count up to ten in Welsh, & have learnt a few expressions. It will soon be time to milk the cows now. I can milk a bit. I drink buttermilk for dinner, & have cream on the stewed fruit. Indeed I fare very sumptuously, & I wish Mary was here to eat the plums we get off the tree every day. There are nine little piggies. You would be amused if you saw them. Their heads are too large for their bodies & their tails are like curly bits of string.

We are having fine weather now I am very glad of the boots, because in the morning the grass is wet. I have not been to Ruthin yet. When I go I want to buy a little tiny boat to sail down the Clwyd. It is nearly time for the post now.

With love & kisses always
from
Wilfred.

# Ruthin

## *Walter Savage Landor (1775-1864)*

*"It (Ruthin) is really in all respects most delightful . . .Magnificent trees, the richest valley in the world and the most varied hills, with lofty mountains not too near nor too far."*

*So wrote the poet and prose stylist Walter Savage Landor while visiting his friend the philanthropist Joseph Ablett at the latter's home in 1832.*

*Ablett erected his own tombstone, in order, according to Landor, "to induce other people to overcome their prejudices against this situation". This prompted Landor to compose these lines:*

### *Earth!*

O parent in thy retreats
My heart with holier fervour beats,
And fearlessly, thou knowest well,
Contemplates the sepulchral cell.

Guard parent earth, those trees, those flowers
Those refuges from wintery hours
Where every plant from every clime
Renews with joy its native prime.
Long may the fane o'er this lone sod
Lift its meek head toward its God,
And gather, round the tomes of Truth
Its bending elds and blooming youth.
And long too may the binders wave
O'er timely and untimely grave
But, if the virtuous be thy pride,
Keep this one tomb unoccupied.


# Ruthin

## *Leigh Hunt (1784-1859)*

*The poet and essayist Leigh Hunt published several journals supporting the Radical cause. This resulted in him being incarcerated in prison for two years, because of comments which he made about the Prince of Wales.*

*In 1835, in poor health, he took up the suggestion of a stay Rhyl. While there he met the philanthropist Joseph Ablett who invited Hunt to stay at his home, Llanbedr Hall, near Ruthin. Below are extracts from his writings which were directly prompted by the visit.*

'To come into the Vale of Clwyd is to realise the dreams of books . . .
. . . 'Mr Ablett's is a very fine house, with very fine grounds, situate in a most beautiful country like a garden, with the gentle Welsh mountains framing the picture all round you . . . Yesterday in our way from Bodryddan, we stopped and had a second lunch at Denbigh, a place rising on a mount out of the valley, and crowned with the ruins of a fine old castle, which we inspected. We then come hither through Ruthin . . . The whole of this district is intersected with gently undulating fields of grass and corn, etc., with beautiful trees, and hedgerows, except towards Rhyl where the sea-shore commences.'

He also composed the following untitled poem:

'Quilting dear friends with homeward care
In the sweet land that held the Druid,
I touch'd at thee, Llanbedr fair,
Thou lily of the Vale of Clwyd.

Gardens I saw, home's fringes bright, —
A homestead Church, and pastoral valleys
And mountains green of gentle might,
Luring ascent with leafy alleys.

A page from out a Poet's book
It was, — choice Nature's adorning. —
A landscape worth an angel's look, —
A landscape of God on Eden's morning.'


# Ruthin

## *Washington Irving (1783-1859)*

*See note under The River Alun.*

### *From "The Sketch Book"*

The custom of decorating graves was once universally prevalent: osiers
were carefully bent over them to keep the turf uninjured, and about them
were planted evergreens and flowers . . . This usage has now become
extremely rare in England; but it may still be met with in the churchyards
of retired villages among the Welsh mountains, and I recollect an instance
of it at the small town of Ruthin, which lies at the head of the beautiful
Vale of Clwyd . . . In North Wales the peasantry kneel and pray over the
graves of their deceased friends for several Sundays after the internment;
and where the tender rite of strewing and planting flowers is still
practised, it is always renewed on Easter, Whitsuntide, and other
festivals, when the season brings the companion of former fertility more
vividly to mind.

# Denbigh

## Thomas Churchyard (1520-1604)

*Churchyard's home town was Shrewsbury. "The Worthiness of Wales" is a lenghty topographical poem deriving from a tour of both North Wales and the southern counties.*

### From "The Worthiness of Wales" (1587)

O Denbigh now appeare, thy turne is next,
I need no gloss, nor shade to set thee out:
For if my pen doe follow playnest text,
And passe right way, and goe nothing about,
Thou shalt be knowne, as worthie well thou art,
The noblest soyle that is in any part:
And for thy seate and castle do compare,
With any one of Wales, what ere they are.


# Denbigh

## Dr Samuel Johnson (1709-1784)

*See notes under Penmaenmawr, St Asaph.*

### From "A Diary of a Journey into North Wales in the year 1774"

'We dined with Mr Myddleton, the clergyman, of Denbigh, where I saw harvest-men very decently dressed after the afternoon service, standing to be hired. On other days, they stand at about four in the morning. They are hired from day to day.'

'The Castle, with its whole enclosure, has been a prodigious pile; it is now so ruined that the form of the inhabited part cannot easily be traced. There are, as in all old buildings, said to be extensive vaults, which the ruins of the upper works cover and conceal, but into which boys sometimes find a way . . . We saw a church, which was once the chapel of the Castle but is used by the town: it is dedicated to St Hilary . . . At a small distance is the ruin of a church said to have been begun by the great Earl of Leicester, and left unfinished at his death. There was a stone in the

*Denbigh castle*

wall, over the doorway, which it was said would fall and crush the best scholar in the diocese. One Price would not pass under it. They have taken it down.'

# Denbigh

## *Sir Richard Colt Hoare (1758-1838)*

*See under Caernarfon, Llangollen.*

### *From "The Journeys of Sir Richard Colt Hoare through England and Wales" (1793-1810)*

*Saturday 6th June 1801.* My morning was employed in taking views of Denbigh Castle and in visiting the neighbouring church at Whitchurch which contains some interesting monuments. This (according to Pennant) is the parish church of Denbigh . . . The town of Denbigh has a very picturesque appearance as seen from the road to St Asaph. Immediately after my arrival I walked out in search of the most advantageous points of view and encircled the castle. I fixed my point at last from the limestone quarries on the road leading to St Asaph. Here the town appears to very great advantage: the ruins of a fine castle at the summit, the modern church and by its side that of one in ruins (or rather begun but never completed), a fine rich country terminated in mountains at a distance with a very good and broken foreground, and the town covering the declivities of a steep hill, well blended with trees. The whole forms a rich picturesque scene, worthy of the pencil of a Poussin, and similar in many respects to those he chose for his pencil.

# Denbigh

## S. T. Coleridge (1772-1834)

*See under Bala, Abergele, Llangollen.*

At Denbigh is a ruined Castle — it surpasses every thing I could have conceived — I wandered there an hour and a half last evening (this is Tuesday Morning). Two well drest young men were walking there — Come — says one — I'll play my flute — 'twill be romantic! Bless thee for the thought, Man of Genius & Sensibility! I exclaimed — and pre-attuned my heartstring to tremulous emotion. He sat adown (the moon just peering) amid the most awful part of the Ruins — and — romantic Youth! struck up the affecting Tune of *Mrs Casey*' . . . 'Tis fact upon my Honor!

# Denbigh

## Gerald Hanley Hopkins (1844-1889)

*One day in February, 1875, Hopkins walked from St Beunos, at Tremeirchion to Denbigh with a friend. In his journals he describes the town as it is approached from a northerly direction.*
*See under St Asaph, Elwy Valley, Maentwrog, Rhyl.*

'Denbigh is a taking picturesque town. Seen from here it is always beautiful. The limekiln under a quarried cliff on this side of the town is always sending out a white smoke and this, and the greyer smoke of Denbigh, creeping upon the hill, what with sun and wind give fairy effects which are always changing.

The day was bright, the sun sparkling through a frostfog which made the distance dim and the stack of Denbigh hill, as we came near, dead mealy grey against the light: the castle ruins, which crown the hill, were punched out in arches and half arches by bright breaks and eyelets of daylight. We went up to the castle but not in: standing before the gateway I had an instress which only the true old work gives . . . We went to eat our lunch at a corner opening by a stone stile upon a wilderness by which you get down to the town, under the outer wall, overgrown with ivy, bramble, and some graceful herb with glossy bush green sprays, something like celery.'

# Denbigh

## *Askew Roberts*

*The following brief passage reveals quite a lot concerning the public attitude to mental illness in the nineteenth century. Roberts' book appeared in the eighteen eighties.*

### *From "The Gossiping Guide To Wales"*

The Castle grounds are kept in excellent order by the Corporation, and afford — to the sojourners at Rhyl and other places adjacent — a favourite lounging place. Indeed, beauties in the fine prospect from the ruins have been discovered which our forefathers lacked the privilege of witnessing. "My goodness," said a resident lady one day to a tourist family she was conducting through the grounds, "I forgot to bring my glass, or you could have seen the lunatics walking beautifully in the grounds of the asylum!" And, we are bound to say, the visitors lamented the loss they sustained!

# Denbigh

## *Beatrix Potter (1866-1943)*

*Beatrix Potter stayed at Denbigh during the summer of 1895. Her uncle, Frederick Burton, owned Gwaenynog, a large house on the outskirts of the town, and it is interesting to note that members of the family still live there.*
*Young Beatrix was fascinated by a walled kitchen garden, where she would watch the gardener at work. She drew on these recollections when she came to write her immortal "Tale of the Floppy Bunnies". (The gardener became the fictional Mr McGregor). Gwaenynog also has associations with Dr Johnson and Thomas Pennant.*

### *From "The Journals of Beatrix Potter: 1881-1897"*

I could not exactly determine what distinguished the Welsh type, but it is marked, particularly among the women and girls; something about the forehead, eyes, and the fall of the nose, and a rather vacant mouth, a perfect mouse-face sometimes. They all wrinkle up their eyes as though in a strong light, the eyebrows usually arched, the forehead round and the nose long. Dark or blue eyes, red or black hair, an occasional fair, fat type, rather idiotic.

There are no shutters to the house for serious crime, but a farmer who overturned in his gig was picked up by the market people, but a considerable sum of loose money which rolled from his pockets was not forthcoming.

The race is said to be deteriorated by much intermarriage. The Denbigh Asylum seemed populous. I thought it very singular that the lunatics should walk in the Park and come up to the garden-railings. I saw a party of perhaps twenty, with keepers, which I at first took for a cricket match.

My aunt seemed to consider the old women amusing. One had appeared and stopped to tea in the servant's-hall. There is a standing reward of five shillings for strayed ones, not worth the risk in my opinion. A man had knocked at the back door and much bewildered Polly by talking about Mr Gladstone. He fortunately took himself off and presently the keeper arrived in search of him.

Another individual, described as very dangerous and prepared to kill anybody, got into Miss Foster's garden, and being after dark could not be found, so a watch was set in the house, and the following morning he was found sitting among the potatoes, very damp.

These pleasing incidents were scattered over several years, but in my opinion they constitute a drawback to the neighbourhood. I should not care to live amongst the same natives either, it is an uncomfortable, suspicious state when so few can understand English. The climate also I did not like, extremely muggy and relaxing, though no doubt it was aggravated by the thunder.

It is rich, undulating country, woods and pastures, all up and down, the hills really high, but lumpy: not definitely fine landscape but beautiful in detail, especially the den below the house, where there is a little glaring-white cottage buried in wood, sacred to the memory of Dr Johnson. A winding path up the dell leads to an urn erected to that worthy's memory before his death, which seems to have provoked his commonsense.

We had a picnic-tea down at Dr Johnson's, provided by Polly, a very taking young woman, tall, thin and freckled. She made a most excellent treacle-pudding which, combined with the thunder, had disastrous effects upon Alice and me, and finally Polly herself, who took to her bed with two pills and a seidlitz-powder. I should doubt if the air suits young people.

The garden is very large, two-thirds surrounded by a red-brick wall with many apricots, and an inner circle of old grey apple trees on wooden espaliers. It is very productive but not tidy, the prettiest kind of garden, where bright old fashioned flowers grow amongst the currant bushes.

Outside in the straggling park, beyond the great oak trees, were two large quarries where I found many fossils, corals, encrinites and a few shells. One of the latter of obstinate hardness led to an acquaintance with John Evans, who chipped it down most neatly and said it was very natural. He worked in a large shed between carpenter's chips and an anvil, a little wizened, warped Welshman who looked at things sideways with one eye and talked a laboured foreign English. He also had been terrified by uncle Fred's driving, having gone to the mountain on the back seat of the trap.

On the last afternoon we had our excursion to Whit Church. It is the old parish church and burying-ground, and contains a fine alabaster painted monument of a knight, and his lady, recumbent with his feet on an heraldic lion which the stupid Welsh Sexton described as a beast that was killed at the Castle.

The state of the Church was most singular, long deserted, but not dismantled. The flags over the vaults looked almost unsafe to stand on, long green stains of damp trickled down the walls, the high pew-doors hung sideways on their hinges, but still bore legibly the names and crests of those long dead who had worshipped in them.

The carving was rather fine in its dilapidation, and some old Bibles and tattered scutcheons lay about, mouldy and forlorn.

Coming home up through the long hill through Denbigh we heard, through an open window, several young people singing *The Men of Harlech* with great animation, their clear fresh voices like the rippling of a stream. There is a frank ring in this their natural air, which is not any where else to be noted in their un-Englishness.

# Denbigh

## *John Moore (1907-1967)*

*See under Rhyl.*

### *From "Tramping Through Wales" (1931)*

At Denbigh I ate bread-and-cheese at an inn; and there I met a man from Liverpool who had climbed with Mallory and for whom, as for me, Mallory was still one of the Heroes. And so we talked of rocks and mountains and Alpine ice until three o'clock struck and the landlord turned us out.

The result of all this talk about climbing was that I drank much more beer than I should otherwise have done; and as a consequence of that I seemed to stride half-way to St Asaph with seven-league boots, and to drag myself for the other part with feet as heavy as lead. When the fine ecstasy left me I felt muzzy sick; and I had an incipient blister on my heel which hurt me at every step.

*St Asaph*

# St Asaph

## *Daniel Defoe (1660-1731)*

*See under Conwy, Snowdonia, Bangor, Holywell, Vale of Clwyd, Penmaenmawr.*

### *From "A Tour Through The Whole Island of Great Britain"*

. . . we came to St Asaph, a small city, with a cathedral, being a bishopric of tolerable good value . . . It is but a poor town, and ill-built, though the country is so pleasant and rich round it.

# St Asaph

## Joseph Cradock

### From "Ac Account of Some of the Most Romantic Parts of North Wales" (1775)

The city of St Asaph is called in British Llanelwy, on account of its situation in the conflux of the River Elwy with the Clwyd; and St Asaph by the English from its patron Asaph, who in the year 560 erected a Bishops See there. The Bishop of this diocese has no entire county under his jurisdiction, but parts only of the counties of Flint, Denbigh, Montgomery, Merioneth and Salop. The cathedral is a mean structure, and the houses in general but ill built, St Asaph however may boast that it stands in the delightful Vale of Clwyd, though by no means in the finest part of it.

# St Asaph

## Dr Samuel Johnson (1709-1784)

*See note under Penmaenmawr, Denbigh.*

### From "A Journey of a Journey Into North Wales in the year 1774"

We went to Bach y Graig, where we found an old house, built 1567, in an uncommon and incommodious form. My Mistress (Mrs Thrale) chattered about cleaning, but I prevailed on her to go to the top. The floors have been stolen: the windows are stopped.

The house was less than I seemed to expect; the river Clwyd is a brook with a bridge of one arch, about one third of a mile.

The woods have many trees, generally young; but some which seem to decay. They have been lopped. The house never had a garden. The addition of another storey would make a useful house, although it cannot be great. Some buildings which Clough, the founder, intended for warehouses, would make store-chambers and servants' rooms. The ground seems to be good. I wish it well.

# St Asaph

## W. Hutton

*See also under Conwy.*

### From "Remarks Upon North Wales, being the Result of Sixteen Tours of the Principality" 1803

This is the sister city to Bangor, and, like that, consists of one short street, rises a hill, and has seventy-two houses. A man need not travel *over* the city to see it; he may do that while standing still. Nor can he say his eyes are offended with multitude, or his ears with sound.

Here, however, permit me to blazon the kindness of "Mine hostess, at the inn," who, because one half of my family were too much indisposed to eat, would not charge any thing for supper.


# St Asaph

## Felicia Hemans (1793-1835)

*Although born in Liverpool Mrs Hemans spent a large part of her life in North Wales, and from 1809 until 1831 lived at St Asaph.*
*Although most of her verse is probably not read very much today her poem "Casabianca" has the dubious distinction of being among the most parodied in the English language. It opens into the very well known lines:*
*"The boy stood on the burning deck*
*Whence all about had fled."*
*Her love of Wales is revealed in the poem below.*

### Written in North Wales

Oh! happy regions of delight and joy,
And much-loved scenes of bliss without alloy;
Hail! to your mountains, groves, and woodlands dear,
Hail! to your flowery lawns and streamlets clear;
Hail! to your lowly cots and stately parks,
And hail! your meadows green and soaring larks.
Observe yon verdant fields and shady bowers,
Wherein I've passed so many happy hours;

See, too, yon rugged hill, upon whose brow
Majestic trees and woods aspiring grow.
There to the right, the vale of Clwyd ends,
Here to the left, huge Penmaen Mawr extends:
Look to the south, the Cambrian mountains o'er,
Hark! to the north, the ocean's awful roar.
Remark those lowing herds and sportive sheep,
And watchful shepherds too, their flocks who keep.
Behold yon ships, now on the glassy main,
Which spread the sails, their destined port to gain.
These lovely prospects, how they cheer my soul,
With what delight and joy I view the whole!
Accept, Great GOD, thanks for these blessings giv'n,
And may my gratitude ascend to heaven.

# St Asaph

## *Gerard Manley Hopkins (1844-1889)*

*Hopkins, who was born in Essex, was converted to Roman Catholicism under
the influence of Newman, and from 1874 to 1877 was a Jesuit theology student at St
Beuno's college at Tremeirchion, near St Asaph. He felt a deep affinity with Wales and
the Welsh: "I have always looked on myself as half Welsh and so I warm to them." He
became interested in Welsh poetry and, as well as trying to write in Welsh, he adapted some
of the sound patterns associated with the different kinds of cynghanedd in his English
poems. Much of his most ecstatic work was inspired by the landscape of the vale of Clwyd.
Below are two of his poems from that period, followed by some random prose extracts.
See also under Maentwrog, Denbigh, The Elwy Valley, Rhyl.*

### *Hurrahing in Harvest*

Summer ends now; now, barbarous in beauty, the stooks rise
Around; up above, what wind-walks! what lovely behaviour
Of silk-sack clouds! has wilder, wilful-wavier
Meal-drift moulded ever and melted across skies?

I walk, I lift up, I lift up heart, eyes,
Down all that glory in the heavens to glean our Saviour;
And, éyes, heárt, what looks, what lips yet gave you a
Rapturous love's greeting of realer, of rounder replies?

And the azurous hung hills are his world-wielding shoulder
Majestic — as a stallion stalwart, very-violet-sweet! —
These things, these things were here and but the beholder
Wanting; which two when they once meet,
The heart réars wíngs bold and bolder
And hurls for him, O half hurls earth for him off under his feet.

### Moonrise (Denbighshire)

I awoke in the Midsummer not-to-call night, in the white
    and the walk of the morning:
The moon, dwindled and thinned to the fringe of a fingernail
    held to the candle,
Or paring of paradisaïcal fruit, lovely in waning but
    lustreless,
Stepped from the stool, drew back from the barrow, of dark
    Maenefa the mountain;
A cusp still clasped him, a fluke yet fanged him entangled
    him, not quit utterly.
This was the prized, the desirable sight, unsought, presented
    so easily,
Parted me leaf and leaf, divided me, eyelid and eyelid of slumber.


August, 1874

'The house (St Beuno's) stands on a steep hillside, it commands the long-drawn valley of the Clwyd to the sea, a vast prospect, and opposite is Snowdon and its range, just now it being bright visible but coming and going with the weather. The air seems to me very fresh and wholesome. Holidays till the 2nd of October. After that hours of study very close — lectures in dogmatic theology, moral ditto, canon law, church history, scripture, Hebrew and what not. I have half a mind to get up a little Welsh; all the neighbours speak it. I have said nothing about the house. It is built of limestone, decent outside, skimping within, Gothic, like Lancing College done worse. The staircases, galleries, and bopeeps are inexpressible: it takes a fortnight to learn them. pipes of affliction convey luke-warm water of affliction to some of the rooms, others more fortunate have fires. The garden is all heights, terraces, Excelsiors, misty mountain tops, seats up trees called Crows' Nests, flights of steps seemingly up to heaven lined with burning aspiration upon aspiration of scarlet geraniums: it is very pretty and airy but it gives you the impression that if you took a step farther you would find yourself somewhere on Penlimmon, Conway Castle, or Salisbury Craig.'

September, 1874

'With William Kerr, who took me up a hill behind ours (ours is Mynefyn), a furze-grown and healthy hill, from which I could look round the whole country, up the valley towards Ruthin and down to the sea. The cleave in which Bodfari and Caerwys lie was close below . . . The heights of Snowdon were hidden by the clouds . . . Looking all round but most in looking far up the valley I felt an instress and charm of Wales. Indeed in coming here I began to feel a desire to do something for the conversion of Wales. I began to learn Welsh too.'

# The Elwy Valley

## *Gerard Manley Hopkins (1844-1889)*

*The Elwy Valley is situated some five miles from St Asaph. It is a well wooded limestone valley of great beauty where some highly significant prehistoric artifacts have been discovered within recent years. During his period at St Beunos College, a few miles away, Hopkins was a frequent visitor. His excurtions are celebrated in what must surely be one of the finest of all landscape poems.*

*See note under St Asaph, Denbigh, Maentwrog, Rhyl.*

### *In the Valley of the Elwy*

I remember a house where all were good
　To me, God knows, deserving no such thing:
　Comforting smell breathed at very entering,
Fetched fresh, as I suppose, off some sweet wood.
That cordial air made those kind people a hood
　All over, as a bevy of eggs the mothering wing
　Will, or mild nights the new morsels of Spring:
Why, it seemed of course; seemed of right it should.

Lovely the woods, waters, meadows, combes, vales,
All the air things wear that build this world of Wales;
　Only the inmate does not correspond:
God, lover of souls, swaying considerate scales,
Complete thy creature dear O where it fails,
　Being mighty a master, being a father and fond.

Of the Elwy Valley Hopkins wrote in a letter:

'The woods, thick and silvered by sunlight and shade, by the smooth banking of the tree tops expressing the slope of the hill, came down to the green bed of the valley. Below, at a little timber bridge, I looked at some delicate flying shafted ashes and there was one especially of single sonnet-like inscape, between which the sun sent straight bright slenderish panes of silvery sunbeams down the slant towards the eye . . . '

# Corwen

## *Julius Rodenberg (1831-1914)*

*See under Aber, Betws-y-coed.*

### *From "An Autumn in Wales" (1856)*

Then I came to Corwen, a small town, built under overhanging cliffs. Here once again nature has created on a gigantic scale; here the last rocky walls of the highlands tower up against the softer lowlands. In the churchyard is a stone cross in a round stone — both tossed here by a giant, as the guide told me. The place is named Corwen from Cor-vaen, meaning a cross on a stone. The rock towering above the churchyard is called 'Owen Glyndwr's Seat'. In the church wall I was shown a small secret door, locked for centuries, through which the bold rebel often went into the church when he wanted to pray. From here starts the classical territory of the last revolt — the valley of the Dee, the black water, which flows away under thick dark trees to Llangollen and then empties into the sea at Chester. Just beyond Corwen, on the left there is a hill, quite flat on top and planted with pines. It is called Glyndwr's hill. His castle once stood here. The whole valley is full of memories of him. Just as nature has erected here the last granite masses of the highlands, so too does history impart to this land the last and saddest memories of old Wales.

# Corwen

## A. G. Bradley

*See under Llanrwst, Abererch, Bangor.*

### *From "In Praise of North Wales" (1898)*

A fine old stone bridge of several arches crosses the Dee just beyond into the village of Llansaintffraid, now generally called Carrog, which straggles picturesquely along the crown of the river's high and leafy bank. It was a sweet place in harmony with its charming site when I used to frequent it, in various primitive quarters years ago, and harboured many quaint characters, including a venerable bard, who was the quaintest of them all. Some terrible red brick erections have now smirched it most deplorably; and red brick, for some inscrutable reason, refuses to mellow in North Wales. Here, too, survives a decrepit little fourteenth-century stone cottage known as Cachardy Owain, or "Owen's prison". For it was within its narrow walls during those long years of war that he confined two or three of his most formidable enemies whom he had the good luck to capture early. Owen is the national hero of the average Welshman. But he is more of a personage in the memories of folks living here on the Dee, than he is beyond the Berwyns. For though this was his secondary residence, it was in the heart of his property and gave him his name. All the old men hereabouts who used to talk about Glyndwr when I first knew the country, are dead. They had some achievements of his to relate that were hardly scientific history. I would not swear there was not a veteran or two that did not claim to have known him personally!

We are now in the open and meadowy vale of Edeyrnion. Corwen is but two miles distant, and the Dee assumes a rather different character, which it maintains all the way up to Bala Lake; sweeping in broad curves through a flat and verdant vale, now pressing to the foot of the Berwyns to receive some brawling brook from the high recesses of their wild glens, now curving away northward to the base of the less lofty but picturesque and broken hills that face them. Corwen is a typical North Welsh market town, grey and severe, with no aesthetic ambitions of any description. Nor have the needs of the visitor or tripper, as at Llangollen, set any mark upon it. What patches of red brick, always so dreadful against the grey stone of Wales, disturb the eye are purely native effort. It has a quite time-honoured hotel in its spacious market-place which is, of course, the "Owen Glyndwr". It flourished through the coaching period and had its windows regularly broken in sanguinary elections, when some outsider had the hardihood to oppose the stout-fisted combatants of the "Syr Watkin" interest. But what were a few panes of glass in the election expenses of those halcyon days? There is also an interesting old church dedicated to St Sulien. It bears on its north wall the imprint of Glyndwr's dagger, which a hardy legend maintains that he flung in a rage from the top of Pen-pigin — a throw of about three-quarters of a mile as the crow flies!

The little town is tucked right under the rather sharp northern rampart of the Berwyns, which, though giving a touch of the picturesque to its austerity, deprives it, as in the case of Llangollen, of its due share of sunlight. The grouse moors hang so close above it that on a shooting day a towering bird might easily drop dead in the High Street. Unpretentious as it looks on an off-day, it is a great gathering-place for both hill and valley men. At its cattle and sheep markets it is alive with rustic humanity all talking Welsh, mostly with animation. When the preachers muster here in force and hold a Calvinistic Methodist or Baptist festival, the hills and vales swarm into it again to hear sermons and to sing hymns. The Welsh Church, as every one knows, is now disestablished and deprived of its endowments. The process might be described as "expedient spoliation."

# Llangollen

## *Sir Richard Colt Hoare (1758-1838)*

*For notes see under Caernarfon, Denbigh.*

## *From "The Journeys of Sir Richard Colt Hoare: 1773-1810"*

The remains of the celebrated abbey in Vale Crucis are about two miles distant and, though not so well preserved as their beautiful architecture should have merited, still merit the attention of every traveller who will view them as an artist or antiquarian. To the former they will afford much employment for his pencil. The ruins are surrounded by fine old ash trees whose delicate taper corresponds well with the elegant light Gothic architecture of the building, but I could wish one or two of them removed to admit a more perfect view of the fine western front. This abbey, formerly the residence of a numerous fraternity of *(Cistercian monks)* is now converted into a farmhouse. The modern buildings intermixed with the old architecture have not a bad effect. A little rapid brook runs near it. It is backed by a lofty mountain covered with fine wood and the situation is such as the monks generally selected for their habitations; who in this respect at least knew how to mix the *utile* with the *dulce*: a good soil, fine water, and a sheltered and secluded spot.

# Llangollen

## *William Hazlitt (1778-1830)*

*Hazlitt was one of the finest critics and essayists of the Romantic period. The vigour and individuality of his work make him highly readable for modern readers.*
*He spent his twentieth birthday at Llangollen, and recalled the visit a mixture of pleasure and melancholy.*

### *From "On Going A Journey"*

It was on the 10th of April 1790 that I sat down to a volume of the "New Eloise", at the inn at Llangollen, over a bottle of sherry and a cold chicken. The letter I chose was that in which St Preux describes his feelings as he first caught a glimpse from the heights of the Jura of the Pays de Vaud, which I had brought with me as a *bon bouche* to crown the evening with. It was my birthday, and I had for the first time come from a place in the neighbourhood to visit this delightful spot. The road to Llangollen turns off between Chirk and Wrexham; and on passing a certain point you come all at once upon the valley, which opens like an amphitheatre, broad, barren hills rising in majestic state on either side, with "green upland swells that echo to the bleat of flocks" below, and the river Dee babbling over its stony bed in the midst of them. The valley at this time "glittered green with sunny showers", and a budding ash-tree dipped its tender branches in the chiding stream. How proud, how glad I was to walk along the highroad that overlooks the delicious prospect, repeating the lines which I have just quoted from Mr Coleridge's poems! But besides the prospect which opened beneath my feet, another also opened to my inward sight, a heavenly vision, on which were written, in letters large as Hope could make them, these four words, LIBERTY,

GENIUS, LOVE, VIRTUE, which have since faded into the light of common day, or mock my idle gaze.

"The beautiful is vanished, and returns not."

Still, I would return some time or other to this enchanted spot; but I would return to it alone. What other self could I find to share that influx of thoughts, of regret, and delight, the fragments of which I could hardly conjure up to myself, so much have they been broken and defaced? I could stand on some tall rock, and overlook the precipice of years that separates me from what I then was. I was at that time going shortly to visit the poet whom I have above named. Where is he now? Not only I myself have changed; the world, which was then new to me, has become old and incorrigible. Yet will I turn to thee in thought, O sylvan Dee, in joy, in youth and gladness, as thou then wert; and thou shalt always be to me the river of Paradise, where I will drink of the waters of life freely!

# Llangollen

## *Samuel Taylor Coleridge (1772-1834)*

*The word clapped in this passage is a reference to sexual disease.*
*See under Bala, Abergele, Denbigh.*

### *In a letter to Robert Southey (1794)*

From Bala we travelled onward to Llanvollin (Llangollen), a most beautiful Village in a most beautiful situation. On the Road we met the Cantabs of my College, Brooke & Berdmore — these rival *pedestrians*, perfect *Powells*, were vigorously pursuing their tour — in a *post chaise*! We laughed famously — their only excuse was, that Berdmore had got *clapped*.

# Llangollen

## *Anne Grant (1755-1838)*

*This Scottish poet and critic wrote the following poem in tribute to the Ladies of Llangollen, Lady Eleanor Butler and Miss Sarah Ponsonby, following a visit:*

In the Vale of Llangollen a Cottage is seen
Well shelter'd from tempests by shades ever green
Where the daisy first opens its eye — to the day
And the hawthorn first flowers on the bosom of May.

There far from the haunts of ambition and pride
Contentment, and virtue, and friendship abide,
And nature, complacent smiles sweet on the pair
Who have splendour forsaken to worship her there.

Bright patterns of wisdom affection and truth
Retired to the shade in the gay bloom of youth
Your sweet rural cottage and pastoral views
Are the charm of the Vale, and the theme of the Muse.

To the Shade for concealment in vain you retire,
We follow to wonder — to gaze — and admire.
Those graces which fancy, and feeling refine,
Like the glow-worm thro' deepest obscurity shine.

While ambition exults in her storm-beaten dome,
Like the tower on your Mountain that frowns o'er your home
With tranquil seclusion, and friendship your lot
How blest, how secure, and how envied your cot!

*Valle Crucis Abbey, near Llangollen*

# Llangollen

## *Louis Simond (1767-1831)*

*Simond was a Frenchman who lived in America for some twenty years. In 1809 he arrived in England where he remained for two years. His account of his experiences were written in English.*
*He was one of the many visitors to Plas Newydd, the home of the Ladies of Llangollen.*

### *From "Journal of a Tour and Residence in Great Britain during the years 1910 and 1811"*

Near Llangollen, where we dined, is the residence of two ladies, whose names are identified with the vale, Lady E. Butler and Miss Ponsonby; and after having informed ourselves of the etiquette of the place, we dispatched a note requesting permission to see the grounds, announcing ourselves, in hopes of strengthening our claim, as American travellers. The ladies, however, were cruel, and answered, 'it was not convenient to permit the place to be seen that day'. The landlady, who had overheard some words of French spoken among us, observed that the ladies were fond of the French language, and that, if we had petitioned in French, we should have been admitted. The hint came too late . . .

. . . French readers may wish to learn something of these ladies. Their story is understood to be, that with birth, beauty, and fortune, they embraced, in the prime of their youths, half a century ago, the romantic idea of consecrating the remainder of their lives to pure friendship, far from the world, its vanities, its pleasures, and its pains; and, literally running away from their families in Ireland, with a faithful woman-servant, lately dead, they hid themselves in this then profound solitude, where they have lived ever since . . . Llangollen is, like all the little old towns of this and all countries, a hideous object.

# Llangollen

## *William Wordsworth (1770-1850)*

*Wordsworth also visited the Ladies of Llangollen at Plas Newydd. Afterwards he wrote the following lines to which, it seems, the ladies took exception. They disliked his description of their home as "a low roof'd cot".*
*See under Caernarfon, Snowdonia.*

Glyn Cafaillgarock, in the Cambrian tongue,
In ours the Vale of Friendship, let this spot
Be nam'd where faithful to a low roof'd Cot
On Deva's banks, ye have abode so long,
Sisters in love, a love allowed to climb
Ev'n on this earth, above the reach of time.

# Llangollen

## *Felix Mendelssohn (1809-1847)*

*In 1829 Mendelssohn visited his friends the Taylors' at their home ar Rhyd y Mwyn near Mold. He stayed for approximately a week, in the course of which he walked to Caernarfon and Snowdonia.*
*The Taylor sisters plied him with flowers, begging him to compose something especially for*

*them. He did indeed compose three pieces, the best known being the Andante in E Major ('the Rivulet').*
*Prior to his visit to the Taylors he stayed at an inn at Llangollen, and wrote in a very disgruntled way about this experience in what is now a town with a unique reputaion for international music making.*

Ten thousand devils take all national music! Here I am in Wales, and, heaven help us! a harper sits in the hall of every reputable tavern playing so called folk melodies — that is to say, dreadful, vulgar, out-of-tune, trash with a hurdy-gurdy going on at the same time!

It has given me toothache already. Scotch bagpipes. Swiss cow-horns, Welsh harps — all playing the Huntsman's Chorus with hideously improvised variations . . . It's unspeakable. Anyone who, like myself can't stand Beethoven's national songs ought to come to Wales and hear them bellowed by rough nasal voices to the crudest accompliment — and then try to keep his temper. As I write a fellow in the hall is playing . . . it makes me so angry I can't go on.

# Llangollen

## *Francis Kilvert (1840-1879)*

*See under Anglesey, Dolgellau & Cader Idris.*
*Kilvert's comments on the Welsh harp offer a striking contrast to those of Mendelssohn.*

Friday, 16h June.

At 6 o'clock we left Chester for Llangollen. We walked up through the town to the Hand Hotel, stopping a moment on the fine quaint old grey stone bridge of Dee with its sharp angled recesses, to look down into the clear rocky swift winding river, so like the Wye. As we came near the Hand we heard the strains of a Welsh harp, the first I ever heard. The harper was playing in the hall the air 'Jenny Jones'. I would have come all the way to Llangollen on purpose to hear the Welsh harp. This is the only hotel in Wales where a Welsh harper can be heard. I stood by him entranced while he played Llwyn-on and the Roaring of the Valley, and several of the other guests in the house gathered round the harp in the corner of the hall. The harper was a cripple and his crutch rested by his side against a chair. He was a beautiful performer and he was playing on a handsome harp of sycamore and ash, which he had won as a prize at an Eisteddfod. I had a good deal of talk with him after he had done playing. He told me there were very few people now who could play the Welsh and the instrument was fast going out of use. The young people learn the English harp which is much easier being double stringed instead of treble stringed. The Welsh harp has no silver string and it is played from the left shoulder while the English harp is played from the right shoulder. Sir Watkin keeps no harper. His sister does, and her harper is the brother of old Pugh of Dolgelly who took me up Cader Idris. The Llangollen harper said he knew him and though him a good harper, but his brother whom he also knew and who is dead was much better, the first harper in Wales.

Presently the harper covered his harp and limped away to his own house in the town, saying he should come and play again at 9 o'clock. He plays in the hall at several stated hours every day. He gets nothing from the Hotel and subsists entirely on what visitors give him. At 9 o'clock he came again and played while we were at supper. It was a great and strange delight to listen to the music of this Welsh harp. The house was full of the melody of the beautiful Welsh airs. No wonder when the evil spirit was upon Saul and when David played upon the harp, that Saul was refreshed and was well and that the evil spirit departed from him.


# Wrexham


### *George Borrow (1803-1881)*

*See under Snowdonia.*


### *From "Wild Wales" (1862)*

I now saw Wrexham Church at about the distance of three miles, and presently entered a lane which led gently down from the hills, which were the same heights I had seen on my right hand, some months previously, on my way from Wrexham to Rhiwabon. The scenery now became very pretty — hedge-rows were on either side, a luxuriance of trees and plenty of green fields. I reached the bottom of the lane, beyond which I saw a strange-looking house upon a slope on the right hand. It was very large, ruinous and seemingly deserted. A little beyond it was a farm-house,

*Wrexham church*

connected with which was a long row of farming buildings along the road-side. Seeing a woman seated knitting at the door of a little cottage I asked her in English the name of the old ruinous house.

"Cadogan Hall, sir," she replied.

"And whom does it belong to?" said I.

"I don't know exactly," replied the woman, "but Mr Morris at the farm holds it, and stows his things in it."

"Can you tell me anything about it?" said I.

"Nothing further," said the woman, "than that it is said to be haunted and to have been a barrack many years ago."

"Can you speak Welsh?" said I.

"No," said the woman, "I am Welsh but have no Welsh language."

Leaving the woman I put on my best speed and in about half an hour reached Wrexham.

The first thing I did on my arrival was to go to the bookshop and purchase the Welsh methodistical book. It cost me seven shillings, and was a thick bulky octavo with a cut-and-come again expression about it, which was anything but disagreeable to me, for I hate your flimsy publications. The evening was now beginning to set in, and feeling somewhat hungry I hurried off to the Wynstay Arms through streets crowded with market people. On arriving at the inn I entered the grand room and ordered dinner. The waiters, observing me splashed with mud from head to foot, looked at me dubiously; seeing, however, the respectable-looking volume which I bore in my hand — none of your railroad stuff — they became more assured, and I presently heard one say to the other, "It's all right — that's Mr So-and-So, the great Baptist preacher. He has been preaching amongst the hills — don't you see his Bible?"

Seating myself at a table I inspected the volume. And here perhaps the reader expects that I shall regale him with an analysis of the methodistical volume at least as long as that of the life of Tom o' the Dingle. In that case, however, he will be disappointed; all I shall at present say of it is, that it contained a history of Methodism in Wales, with the lives of the principal Welsh Methodists. That it was fraught with curious and original matter, was written in a straightforward methodical style, and that I have no doubt it will some day or other be extensively known and highly prized.

After dinner I called for half a pint of wine. Whilst I was trifling over it, a commercial traveller entered into conversation with me. After some time he asked me if I was going farther that night.

"To Llangollen," said I.

"By the ten o'clock train?" said he.

"No," I replied, "I am going on foot."

"On foot!" said he; "I would not go on foot there this night for fifty pounds."

"Why not?" said I.

"For fear of being knocked down by the colliers, who will be all out and drunk."

"If not more than two attack me," said I, "I shan't much mind. With this book I am sure I can knock down one, and I think I can find play for the other with my fists."

The commercial traveller looked at me. "A strange kind of Baptist minister," I thought I heard him say.

# Wrexham

## H. G. Wells (1866-1946)

*In the first volume of his "Experiment in Autobiography" H. G. Wells describes his experiences as a young teacher at the Holt Academy, near Wrexham, in 1887.*

### From "Experiment in Autobiography"

The Holt Academy, Wrexham seemed, on paper, the most desirable of all the places offered me by the agencies. It was a complex organization. A boys' school plus a girls' school plus a college for the preparation of young men for the Calvinistic Methodist ministry, promised variety of teaching and possibilities of talk and exercise with students of my own age.

I expected a library, playing fields, a room of my own. I expected fresh air and good plain living. I thought all Wales was lake and mountain and wild loveliness. And the Holt Academy had the added advantage of re-opening at the end of July and so shortening the gap of impecuniosity after the College of Science dispersed.

But when I got to Holt I found only the decaying remains of a once prosperous institution set in a dismal street of houses in a flat ungainly landscape. Holt was a small old town shrunk to the dimensions of a village, and its most prominent feature was a gasometer. The school house was an untidy dwelling with what seemed to be a small white-washed ex-chapel, with broken and dirty windows and a brick floor, by way of schoolroom. The girls' school was perhaps a score of children and growing girls in a cramped little villa down the street. The candidates for the ministry were three lumpish young men apparently just off the fields, and the boys' school was a handful of farmers' and shop-keepers' sons. My new employer presented himself as a barrel of a man with bright eyes in a round, ill-shaven face, a glib tongue and a staccato Welsh accent, dressed in the black coat, white tie and top hat deat to Tommy Morley, the traditional garb of the dominie. He was dirty, — I still remember his blackened teeth — and his wife was dirty, with a certain life-soiled prettiness. He conducted me to a bedroom which I was to share, I learnt, with two of the embryo Calvinistic ministers.

My dismay deepened as I went over the premises and discovered the routines of the place. The few boarders were crowded into a room or so, sleeping two and three in a bed with no supervision. My only colleague was a Frenchman, Raut, of whom I heard years afterwards, because he claimed to have possessed himself of the manuscript of a story by me which he was offering for sale. (I found myself unable to authenticate that manuscript). Meals were served in a room upon a long table covered with American cloth and the food was poor and the cooking bad. There was neither time-table nor scheme of work. We started lessons just anyhow. Spasmodic unexpected half-holidays alternated with storms of educational energy, when we worked far into the evening. Jones had a certain gift for eloquence which vented itself in long prayers and exhortatiions at meals or on any odd occasion. He would open school with prayer. On occasions of crisis he would pray. His confidence in God was remarkable. He never hesitated to bring himself and us to the attention of an Avenging Providence. He did little teaching himself, but hovered about and interfered. At times, the tedium of life became too much for him and his wife. He would appear unexpectedly in the schoolroom, flushed and staggering, to make a long wandering discourse about nothing in particular or to assail some casual victim with vague disconcerting reproaches. Then for a day or so he would be missing and in his private quarters, and Raut and I and the theological students would keep such order as we found practicable and convenient.

These theological students aimed at some easy, qualifying examination for their spiritual functions. The chief requirement for their high calling was a capacity for intermittent religious feeling and its expression in Welsh, and that they had by birth and routine. They were instructed in "divinity" (poor God!) and the elements of polite learning when it seemed good to Jones that this should happen. They were not without ambitions. Their hopes, I learnt, were not bounded by their own sect. A qualified minister of the Calvinistic Methodists might sometimes be accepted as a recruit and further polished by — I think it was — the Wesleyans. A Welsh-speaking Wesleyan again might have scruples of conscience and get into the Anglican priesthood. The Anglican priesthood had always openings for Welsh speakers and so, far up the vistas of life, a living in the established church beckoned to my room-mates I know not how far this process of ratting might be carried. An unmarried Anglican can, I believe, become a Roman Catholic priest. In Christendom all roads lead to Rome, and so my room-mates were potential, if highly improbable, popes.

# Hiraethog

## *W. T. Palmer*

*Hiraethog is a remote upland area with a rich historic and cultural past. Geographically it
extends into areas of both Gwynedd and Clwyd.
Palmer's book appeared in 1945.*

### *From "More Odd Corners in North Wales"*

On this desolate moor where Denbigh meets Caernarfon and Merioneth,
great snow-storms have given many heroic incidents and much dreary
labour to men and dogs. As usual, the woman's part has been mainly that
of weary waiting. In many a cot the fire has not been let down, the lamps
have not been quenched, for a week — storm and darkness go together in
mid-winter on the heights.

I have worked with Evan, searching for buried sheep when the
midnight was one howl of storm; and an anxious woman awaited the
delayed return of her storm-battered man. In the cot-house by the hill the
stir of life is still, and the clock beside the door ticks so loud and hopeless
that the wife is tempted to stop its swinging stroke; on the hearth the peat
fire is burning grey, and there is menace in the hollow blast plucking at
window-shutters and booming in the chimney.

The wife of the shepherd must be ready to give hot food and drink at
any hour, for as long as the storm keeps its fiendish grip there must be
rounds to see that the sheep are safe. A mere point in the direction of the
blizzard may mean that a hundred ewes are overwhelmed, that some field
which has hitherto been safe is buried in whirling snow. "While
Shepherds Watch" is much more than a pleasant Christmas sentiment.

Hour after hour the woman sits, staring into the dying fire, unable to
read, with no work to employ her nerveless hands. She knows the terror of
the storm, and perhaps imagines with ever-increasing terror:

In a snow-wreath's weltering deeps
The long-lost shepherd sleeps,
And his sheep-dog from the spot
Wanders not . . .

But there, isn't that a scratch at the door, the claws of old Jeff rushing
for the shelter, with his master following at his tail? Then a man's hand
fumbles at the latch, and the door opens, bringing in a little whirl of snow.

"It's chill work, wife, but the wind's dropping, and there's less of snow every hour. I reckon we can sleep down till daylight without danger to the sheep. It's been pretty bad on the far side of the hill, but the dogs have worked well." And a happy woman raises a song of thankfulness in her heart for danger which has passed, but which is not forgotten.

# Llanrhaeadr-ym-mochnant

## *Henry Skrine*

### *From "Two Successive Tours Throughout the Whole of Wales" (1798)*

Under the conduct of a guide not abounding in intelligence we again scaled the mountains, and pursued a very dreary and uneven track over the Berwins to the wretched village and still more miserable inn of Llanrhaidr, from whence a rugged lane led us to the celebrated cataract of the Pistyll-Rhaidr. Though certainly the highest, this is far from being the most picturesque waterfall we had seen in our tour, and perhaps it fails at the first view to strike the sight so forcibly as might be expected, in consequence of the great defect it labours under in the total want of all external scenery. Here are no leafy groves to relieve the eye, no verdant lawns to smooth the approach, but a narrow valley between two barren hills carried us straight forward to the object of our search, which met our eyes with a disadvantageous sameness of appearance long before we arrived at it. We could not, however, but be impressed with its magnitude when we came upon the spot, though the stream was rather more scanty than usual from a temporary deficiency of water. A lofty barrier of black rocks closes the vale here, from whose summit the torrent descends in a perpendicular but uneven fall of about 150 feet, at the bottom of which it has worn its passage through a ridge of the projecting rock and rushes into the valley through an extraordinary arch of its own making in another descent of near 50 feet. The object was altogether singular and stupendous, and though the peculiar imagery of landscape was wanting, our most sanguine expectations could not but be exceeded by so great a production of nature, which seemed to invade the realms of fancy, and ape the magic drapery of an oriental romance.

# Miscellaneous

## *Louisa Costello*

*See also under Maentwrog, Hawarden, Snowdonia.*

### *"The Falls, Lakes and Mountains of North Wales" (1839)*

It would seem as if that part of the country called "The Principality" had been created by Nature, in a holiday humour, expressly for the recreation and delight of English tourists, whose limited time did not allow them to seek for beauties abroad; for, collected into a small space, more that is graceful, beautiful and romantic, may be found in North Wales than in any other spot in Europe.

I should recommend to the traveller to pursue the route we chose, entering North Wales by Chester, and quitting it by the fine, old town of Shrewsbury; as, by this means, he becomes acquainted with the most striking objects in proper succession, and, after the bold features of the region of Snowdon, he enjoys the more the quiet grace of the vale of Llangollen. Whichever way it may, however, please the wanderer to take, he is certain to be more gratified in this tour than in almost any other on so small a scale: for all the sights of North Wales may be well seen in a month, although we allowed ourselves to finger amongst her valleys and mountains a whole summer.

## *Julius Rodenberg (1831-1914)*

*When this German traveller commenced his Welsh visit at a Liverpool railway station an immediate verbal misunderstanding arose.*
*See also under Aber, Betws-y-coed, Corwen.*

### *From "An Autumn in Wales" (1856)*

' . . . I walked up to the counter and asked for a ticket to Aber — but the official didn't understand me and I had to repeat my request. But that didn't help me either; the man became impatient and I became very embarrassed, for I couldn't understand how a word apparently so simple and consisting of only four letters, could be pronounced any differently than I must have already said it in one of my attempts. However, there was no way of making him understand other than by giving him the name written down, whereupon he himself now spoke, and so deeply and obscurely that even today, after much practice, I would not be sure of getting the right tone. He gave me my ticket, and I was shown into a carriage . . . '

Beyond Chester the mountains came in at once, at first quite distant in a bluish shimmer, while on the right a broad and gently furrowed sandy area with occasional strips of water and even boats stranded at an angle on the dry land, showed that here the sea began and that it was now low tide. As these and similar sights could only be seen through the window beside which the girls were sitting, I also had the opportunity of enjoying the freshness and charm of their faces, and with old Klopstock's verse for an apology:

Mother Nature, the splendour
Of your works, scattered
Over the land, is fine
But a happy face is finer.

At Mostyn the landscape acquired a definite character, unfolding more beautifully and richly, the further our train advanced; indeed, here it reveals in advance what the traveller can expect from the Welsh highlands, where the footpath, like the railway, leads from surprise to surprise between sea and mountain. On our left lay a large luxuriantly green oak wood, from the midst of which on a jutting rock rose a castle looking most picturesque with its white walls in such a lovely setting. Then the view extended out to the open sea, rolling here between the Welsh shore and the coasts of Ireland. I had never made such a journey in my life before; for even the Belgian train from Verviers to Liège, which had charmed me so much, I cannot compare with this. There as here you have the charming green landscape and the mountains, powerfully and picturesquely grouped; but in Wales there is also the sea, and always so close that you think the waves must be lapping the wheels of the engine.

# Rev J. Evans

*Evans' observations on the Welsh rural life of his time make fascinating reading.*

## From "A Tour Through Part of North Wales" (1798)

The men are in general rather below than above the middle stature. They are thickset, with limbs rather small; and though instances have sometimes occurred of prodigious strength, yet, like their ancestors, they are light and active, more free than strong; and the modern, like the ancient Briton, is not very attentive to food or clothing. The latter consists of a flannel jacket and breeches for the men; and a lindsey jacket and petticoat, with a round felt hat, for the women; while both sexes are seen to climb the craggy steep, and trip over the thorny plain naked to the knee. But they are not destitute of shoes and stockings; these they carry in their hands to market and to church; and at the next adjacent stream they sit down on a stone, wash their feet, and put them on. Returning, they perform the same ceremony, and lay them up again. Their food is equally coarse and scanty. Oatmeal cake or barley-bread, and potatoes; and their drink the diodgriafel. This course is sometimes varied by hung-goat, dried fish, cheese made of goats' and sheep's milk, and buttermilk, grown acid from keeping. The cakes are manufactured by the mistress of the house; the meal is made into past with water, and spread thin upon the backstone over the fire, to bake. The colour raises a dislike, otherwise the taste is not disagreeable. Wheat flour may be found in some houses, but, as yeast is rare, there is consequently little fermented bread.

Refinement has not yet deadened the natural feelings of the Welsh, nor produced that apathy of behaviour which prevails among a more polished people. The fondness they evince for their country, and tenacious adherence to their native language, is not more remarkable than their singular attachment for each other. This spirit, which pervades the community, in individuals is most eminently displayed. Zeal for the welfare of every branch of a numerous family, which produces reciprocal protection and respect between the higher and lower classes, frequently calls forth a spirit into action rarely to be met with elsewhere; and has, on some occasions, been exhibited in a manner, that, to those narrow minds which make *self* the centre of every ray of exertion, would appear extravagance and romance. Take one illustration.

In consequence of the poverty of the soil and state of husbandry, the harvest is very late; and frequently, from the uncertain state of the weather, a difficulty occurs of procuring the scanty crops upon which their existence depends. It often happens, that the strength of hands is not adequate to the labour, and a poor farmer is in danger of being ruined. But there is a natural sympathy amongst the Welsh, that provides for this adverse circumstance. Sensible of the evil arising from a scanty crop badly houses, they form societies of assistance, called Cymmorthean Cynhauaf. As soon as one or two farmers have finished their own, or what portion is ready, they immediately repair, with their servants and horses, to assist their backward neighbour. This they do without any other fee or reward than their maintenance, and the consciousness that arises from the performance of an act of brotherly kindness. We have seen numbers engaged in this amiable occupation, and the pleasure they felt might be deduced from their clamorous exultation. If the sky lowers, and gathering clouds forbode a storm, likely to mar their friendly intentions, the noise increases, exertion is redoubled, and they seem more anxious to secure their neighbour's produce than their own. The desirable end accomplished, they return with shouting to the house, where, congratulating the farmer's good fortune, they express their mutual happiness in acts of cheering festivity.

# Acknowledgements

*We are grateful to the following for kindly granting permission for certain poems and prose extracts to appear in this anthology.*

Oxford University Press for letters written by Wilfred Owen, included in *Journey From Obscurity* by Harold Owen

Oxford University Press for *"At A Welsh Waterfall"* and passages from the letters of Gerard Manley Hopkins

Oxford University Press for extracts from *A London Girl in the 1880's* by M. V. Hughes

Frederick Warne for extracts from *The Journal of Beatrix Potter: 1881-1897*

A. P. Watt, on behalf of the literary executors of the estate of H. G. Wells, for an extract from *Experiment in Autobiography* by H. G. Wells

Penguin Books Ltd for extracts from *The Journey Through Wales and the Description of Wales* by Gerald of Wales, translated by Lewis Thorpe (1978)

D Brown and Sons Ltd., Publishers, Eastgate Press, Cowbridge, South Glamorgan, for extracts from *An Autumn in Wales* by Julius Rodenberg, translated by William Linnard

Professor William Tydeman and Professor Alun Jones for extracts from *A Pedestrian Tour of North Wales* by Joseph Hucks

Professor William Tydeman for passages from the works of Walter Savage Landor and Leigh Hunt included in a paper entitled *Joseph Ablett: Patron of the Arts* published in the transactions of the Denbigh-shire Historical Society

Gwasg Gee, Denbigh, for extracts from *Michael Farraday in Wales* edited by Dafydd Tomos

Gwasg Gomer for an extract from *A Spinster's Tour Through North Wales* by Augusta Pearson

Alan Sutton Publishing for extracts from *The Journeys of Sir Richard Colt Hoare through England and Wales: 1773-1810* edited by M. W. Thompson

Weidenfeld and Nicolson for a passage by Shelley, extracted from *Shelley the Pursuit* by Richard Holmes

Methuen for extracts from *In Search of Wales* by H. V. Morton

J. M. Dent for permission to include extracts from *Tramping Through Wales* by John Moore

Clwyd Records Office, Ruthin, for permission to include previously unpublished extracts from the *Journals of William Graeme Tomkins*

C. Morris and the Cresset Press for extracts from *The Journeys of Celia Fiennes*